JB JOSSEY-BASS

First-Time Leaders of Small Groups

How to Create High-Performing Committees, Task Forces, Clubs, and Boards

Manuel London

Marilyn London

John Wiley & Sons, Inc.

Published by Jossey-Bass
A Wiley Imprint
989 Market Street, San Francisco, CA 94103-1741   www.josseybass.com

Readers should be aware that Internet Web sites offered as citations and/or sources for further
information may have changed or disappeared between the time this was written and when it
is read.

Limit of Liability/Disclaimer of Warranty: While the publisher and author have used their best
efforts in preparing this book, they make no representations or warranties with respect to the
accuracy or completeness of the contents of this book and specifically disclaim any implied
warranties of merchantability or fitness for a particular purpose. No warranty may be created
or extended by sales representatives or written sales materials. The advice and strategies
contained herein may not be suitable for your situation. You should consult with a professional
where appropriate. Neither the publisher nor author shall be liable for any loss of profit or any
other commercial damages, including but not limited to special, incidental, consequential,
or other damages.

Jossey-Bass books and products are available through most bookstores. To contact Jossey-Bass
directly call our Customer Care Department within the U.S. at 800-956-7739, outside the U.S.
at 317-572-3986, or fax 317-572-4002.

Jossey-Bass also publishes its books in a variety of electronic formats. Some content that appears
in print may not be available in electronic books.

Library of Congress Cataloging-in-Publication Data

London, Manuel.
     First-time leaders of small groups : how to create high-performing committees, task forces,
clubs, and boards / Manuel London, Marilyn London.—1st ed.
        p. cm.
     Includes bibliographical references and index.
     ISBN 978-0-7879-8650-6 (cloth)
     1. Small groups. 2. Leadership. I. London, Marilyn, 1952- II. Title.
HM736.L66 2007
303.3'4—dc22   2006101885

Printed in the United States of America
FIRST EDITION
HB Printing   10 9 8 7 6 5 4 3 2 1

The Jossey-Bass Business
& Management Series

CONTENTS

PREFACE

This book is for anyone who is, or might soon be, the leader of a small group. You may be the chair of a committee, head of a task force, or president of a club or board. The book is for people who have never led a group before and for experienced leaders who want to improve their techniques or are facing an especially challenging group. The book will help you learn what your group needs from you so that you can be as effective as possible.

If you are leading a committee, task force, club, or board, this book will be of more interest to you than a general book on teams. Leading a small group that meets periodically is different from being a supervisor of an ongoing work group. In an ongoing work group, employees have specific jobs and roles, and the company has policies and procedures for selecting and evaluating employees.

Although there are some common elements of leadership that apply in many team and work group situations, leading a small, short-term group is different. Members often do not have specific roles. The group gets its work done during meetings or through electronic communications. The group process is likely to be free-flowing and unstructured, at least initially. When the group meets for the first time, members may not even know, or agree on, what the group is trying to do, let alone how they are going to do it. Members may vary in their motivation for being in the group and their ability to be a productive, cooperative member of the group. Unlike a natural work team, a short-term group meets periodically—maybe a few times a week, maybe only once a month or even less often. Your task as leader is to make something happen, and do it fast.

The first time you lead a group can be daunting, even if you are an experienced leader. Many people find themselves at the helm with little idea about what to do. If you are in that position, you might ask yourself:

- What can I do to be an effective leader?
- Can I make my group into a high-performing team?
- Can I keep my group members interested and involved?
- Is there a constructive way to raise and resolve conflicts among members?
- How do I deal with difficult members—for instance, people who just don't stop talking or always have to have their way?
- What can I do to help my group learn to be effective quickly?
- What will I learn from this experience that will make me a better leader in the future?

In most organizations, considerable work is accomplished in groups. This applies to for-profit businesses, government, health care, education, and volunteer organizations of all sorts (houses of worship, sports and social clubs, and community service organizations, for example). For instance, large, nonprofit organizations use many volunteer-based committees. Groups do work that one person cannot do alone. Group members may work on complex tasks that require members to depend on each other as they use their expertise and experience to complete a task.

Committees, task forces, and project teams are usually temporary groups, formed to accomplish specific tasks, and they disband when the work is complete. A research and development group may be formed to invent a product or find ways to improve the quality of a product or process. A club may form a subcommittee to plan a fundraising event.

You may belong to multiple groups simultaneously. You may be a leader of one group and a member of others, and your involvement and roles may change over time. You and your group members may have multiple, possibly conflicting, demands on your time. Also, you may have different reasons for being involved in a particular group. Group members may join the same group for different reasons; perhaps they believe in the work, or they want their voice heard, or they were assigned to the group, or they want a chance to socialize with others.

As the leader, you want to recruit people for your group who are motivated and have the expertise you need. You may set the agenda for group meetings, delegate tasks, monitor progress, give members feedback about their performance, find resources, and help members do their jobs. What you do depends in large part on the demands of the task—for instance, the difficulty or complexity of the work, the availability of needed resources, and the time allotted to complete the work. How you lead may also depend on the diversity of the group members' backgrounds and experience and their ability to work together. You may need to be directive and autocratic, especially if the group members have little experience with working in a group. You may find that the best strategy is to involve the group members in all aspects of the group process, encouraging them to participate in discussions and facilitating their making decisions by consensus, meaning that all members understand the issues and are willing to commit to a particular alternative. Ultimately, as leader, you are the one responsible for the group's success or failure.

In writing this book, we drew on our own experiences as leaders, managers, and researchers. We give examples of a wide range of groups and provide clear suggestions for action. Our recommendations are based on research findings in social and organizational psychology about effective leadership strategies and pitfalls to avoid. Our suggestions for assessing your group derive from methods used to investigate group processes and outcomes.

This book has a number of features that will help you in your role as group leader:

- Questions group leaders ask, with answers based on research on what works well and what does not
- Diagnostics for determining your group's current capabilities and need for help
- Leadership challenges—difficulties and barriers that leaders of groups often encounter and ways to overcome them
- Self-assessments to help you consider your strengths and weaknesses and what you can do to build your self-confidence as a group leader
- Examples of different group situations and approaches leaders have taken that had positive and negative results
- Models that will help you understand the way groups work
- Activities you can try to improve the way your group functions
- Key research findings and ideas presented in boxes throughout the book
- Clear suggestions for practice

We have an eight-step process to help you lead your group. These steps are important for any group, but they are especially important for leading short-term groups because you do not have much time to get something done and your members may not be as motivated as you are to make the group successful. The first four steps are for preparing to lead, and the second four are for taking the lead:

Preparing to Lead

Step 1: Identify the type of group you are leading.

Step 2: Create the keys to a high-performing team: talent, time, and task.

Step 3: Plan your group's development.

Step 4: Determine your style of leadership.

Taking the Lead

Step 5: Get off to the right start.

Step 6: Work smart.

Step 7: Help your group learn and get better in the process.

Step 8: Assess your group's progress and achievements.

January 2007   Manuel London

Stony Brook, New York   Marilyn London

For our sons,
David and Jared

ACKNOWLEDGMENTS

We thank the many people who gave us opportunities to participate in, and learn about, groups in organizations. Our knowledge comes from our research and practice. Manny is grateful to the experiences and encouragement he received at AT&T as the company and his position evolved through many iterations of human resource and corporate strategy and at the State University of New York at Stony Brook. In particular, he thanks Ann Howard, Gerrit Wolf, John Marburger, Robert McGrath, Ed Mone, Valerie Sessa, and Thomas Diamante and the late Douglas Bray for their collegiality, professional support, and friendship throughout the years.

Marilyn has spent more than a decade as an administrator for educational support in the Medical School at Stony Brook. She is an active participant in small groups involved in curriculum development and educational planning. As a musician and educator, she has participated in, and studied the interactions of, small musical groups. She is particularly thankful to Peter Williams, Frederick Schiavone, Pierce Gardner, Peter Pece, Elza Mylona, Iris Granek, and Latha Chandran for encouraging her professional development.

ABOUT THE AUTHORS

Manuel London is associate dean of the College of Business, professor of management, and director of the Center for Human Resource Management at the State University of New York at Stony Brook. He previously taught at the University of Illinois at Urbana-Champaign and was a researcher and human resource manager at AT&T. He received his Ph.D. in industrial and organizational psychology from the Ohio State University. His dissertation focused on how small groups make decisions. He has since studied and developed ways to improve individual and group learning. His other Jossey-Bass books include *Maximizing the Value of 360-Degree Feedback* (edited with Walter Tornow), *Developing Managers, Change Agents, Developing the Training Enterprise*, and *Career Management and Survival*. He consults for business and government organizations on group facilitation, performance appraisal, feedback, and career development.

Marilyn London is assistant dean for medical education at the State University of New York at Stony Brook. She holds a doctorate of education with an emphasis in creative arts from Rutgers University and two master's degrees from the University of Illinois at Urbana-Champaign, one in cultural anthropology and the other in piano performance. Her dissertation focused on how small performing groups interact to create high levels of synchronous performance. She has studied and written about tightly integrated groups, such as performance ensembles, with a focus on communication and feedback processes that contribute to group performance among interdependent team members. She has taught graduate courses on diversity, thesis writing, medical ethics, self-awareness, and the use of music to teach basic educational concepts. She has served on and led groups in education and volunteer organizations and has been a member and leader of small musical ensembles as well as large performing groups in which strong teamwork was essential for excellent performance.

Part 1

PREPARING TO LEAD

Chapter 1

IDENTIFYING TYPES OF GROUPS AND THEIR LEADERSHIP CHALLENGES

In this introductory chapter, we provide some examples of what people say about being a group member and leader. We also review how small, short-term groups differ from natural work teams and how different types of short-term groups (committees, task forces, quality improvement teams, clubs, and boards) pose different leadership challenges. For those of you who want to know right away how to get started, the quick start guide in Appendix A is a resource to turn to whenever you begin to lead a new committee or task force. It lists steps to follow to get your group off to the right start, keep members motivated and involved, and be sure you are making progress.

After reading this first chapter, you will be able to:

- Recognize the reasons that members are part of your group and how they feel about it.
- Describe the different kinds of short-term groups and leadership challenges associated with them.
- Distinguish purpose, product, and process.
- Determine the extent to which members in your group need to work together cooperatively to achieve your group's goals.
- Identify different types of groups and the situations they face.
- Diagnose your own group's needs, demands, and challenges.

Let's Begin

When you are asked to chair a small group, lots of questions and concerns undoubtedly run through your mind:

- I've never done this before. Where do I start?
- Who should I select for the group? Should I let people volunteer?
- Am I going to be any good at this? Will the group members listen to me?
- How much of my time will this take?
- How will we spend group meeting time?
- What will I gain from this experience? Will it help my career? What are the risks?
- How important is this anyway to me, my group members, and my department?
- What should I do first?
- How much control over the outcomes should I give up to the group? If the group does a poor job, how will it reflect on me? Will I have to do most of the work?

You may be feeling puzzled, uncertain, and stressed. You're not alone. We'll look at typical reactions people have to being a member of a group and to being a group leader.

Here's what committee and task force leaders say about the challenges they face:

I've been a member of this board for seven years, and I never anticipated being elected president. Since no one else was willing to do it, I agreed. I believe in this organization, and I think my board members do too. Now I just need to get them to work together. We have some excellent paid staff, but our budget is too tight and we need to trim expenses while we raise more money to help the community. [Board president, local nonprofit mental health agency]

My charge is to implement a new online information data retrieval and analysis system to support our global sales staff. To get this done in only six months, I need a project team with technical experts who can work with our consultants to customize the software. I need analysts who will provide the data for the system. Of course, I need representatives of the sales staff to be sure we are designing a product they can use. Also, I need people to write documentation and provide on-site training. This is going to be a massive effort. We will meet regularly, communicate frequently, listen to each other closely, and work fast and hard! [Headquarters sales vice president, international stock trading company]

Everyone on this committee is so different. We're only ten people. Three are older than sixty years of age, and two are under twenty-five. Four are African American, two are Hispanic, one is Asian, and the rest are white. Four are men. Two are very wealthy. How am I ever going to get us to agree on anything? [President, town civic association]

I'm a senior administrative assistant to the principal of a large high school. The principal asked me to chair a committee of faculty to develop ways to introduce problem-based educational modules that require students to draw on their knowledge in different areas to solve problems in groups. I asked, Why me? I have a college education, but I'm not a teacher. My principal wanted someone who is objective and who represents her office to lead the group, so I'm it. I've had to learn to be more assertive than I usually am in order to get the teachers to focus and take this seriously. At first, it was a struggle. Things improved when the principal asked for a presentation on our progress in two weeks. This got everyone's attention, and I was surprised at how helpful the teachers were in showing me how to put together the presentation and then asking me to give it. I'm learning a lot, and I'm getting to know the teachers better, much better than I did before. [School administrative assistant]

Here's what committee and task force members say:

Now I know what people mean when they say, "A camel is a horse designed by a committee." Committees sometimes produce crazy results. You can only wonder, "What were they thinking!?" Everyone has a different perspective. By trying to satisfy everyone, we satisfy no one. [Architect in the facilities department of a large company]

We seem to do everything around here by committee. That's because so many areas need to have their say. It slows everything down. I have to admit, I have little patience. [Bank executive]

Whenever we have a big initiative, such as implementing a new data system, we set up an interdepartmental task force instead of assigning the work to one person or department. These initiatives tend to be complex and touch many different areas. I've learned a lot about how other departments operate by being on these task forces. Also, I've met a lot of people and made friends. This has helped me get my work done. [Telecommunications company manager]

We pull together search committees when we have job vacancies. The committee usually has people from different departments. The committee reviews résumés, interviews candidates, and recommends the top three or four candidates to the hiring supervisor. We do this to ensure that the process is fair and that all applicants have equal opportunity. It's time-consuming, but it works. [University human resource department manager]

These reactions to leading a group and being a member of a group are not unusual. People have mixed experiences. Some are enthusiastic and cooperative. Others are impatient and recalcitrant. Different members' motivation, expertise, and willingness to cooperate with each other are likely to affect what you do as a leader.

You might wonder how to approach the leadership role. Should you be directive, plan meeting agendas, control who speaks when, and make decisions? Should you let the committee members participate actively and almost take over while you serve as facilitator? The answers to these questions depend on the group members—for instance, their capabilities and personalities. The answers also depend on the task—what the group has to get done, by when, and the extent to which group members need structure and direction. How you lead also depends on what you feel comfortable doing, that is, your style of leadership.

This chapter begins the journey of group leadership and creating a high-performance group. It will help you understand the demands on you and your group members. We start by considering different types of groups and your role as leader.

Types of Groups

Now that you have been appointed or elected leader, what type of group is it: a committee, subcommittee, task force, club, or board? You need to understand the characteristics of your group to determine how you are going to lead it.

A group is simply two or more people who work together to accomplish a task. Committees and task forces are often short-term groups that meet periodically. Some of the work is done during meetings and some outside meetings. This book is about small, usually short-term groups. These are different from natural work teams in an organization. Members of natural work teams work together on a regular basis as the central part of each person's job. Team members have specific roles, structured work methods, and ample time to get to know one another. The teams have a clear identity, for instance, the members are all part of the training department.

Short-term groups initially lack identity and cohesion. They do not have extended periods of time to develop issues of values, culture, and coordination (Kozlowski & Ilgen, in press). The members of the group may vary in the extent to which their work is interdependent. Sometimes the members work almost in isolation; the only thing they have in common is their leader. Other times, they work in tight synchrony, as surgery teams, flight crews, and musical ensembles do. Even these teams may vary in composition over time, with members knowing their roles and able to function even if they have not worked together much in the past. The people in such a team know their function and the behaviors they need to carry out.

This book is about temporary groups. They usually disband after the goal is achieved. However, they may have an ongoing function and meet regularly or when needed, but they do not work together on a daily basis. Note that we include clubs, boards, and councils along with committees and subcommittees as small groups. They may not be short term, but members come and go, they meet periodically, they work on short-term projects that have tight deadlines, and what they do may change over time.

Purpose, Product, and Process

There are three key elements to any group: purpose, product, and process. Purpose is the reason for the group's being. Product is the outcome of the group. Process is how the group goes about doing its work. The group's purpose determines the product it produces and the processes it follows. Of course, a group may have more than one purpose and produce more than one product, in which case it may vary its process to suit the particular purpose and product. Groups that do not alter their process to fit their purpose and product may have trouble achieving the desired outcome. Consider the following purposes:

• *Developing vision and strategy.* A group may be formed to create a strategy or vision for an organization. For instance, this may be a long-range planning committee, perhaps a subgroup of a board of directors. The product is a set of goals and action steps that will guide the organization. The process may be to (1) involve board members in discussions about the organization's performance, (2) collect information about the competitive environment today and opinions about changes or conditions on the horizon, (3) conduct a customer survey about their needs and expectations, (4) hold a series of meetings with people who have a stake in the organization (such as clients, suppliers, or members), (5) formulate ideas for future goals and ways of accomplishing them, (6) circulate the draft of goals and strategies and hold open meetings to discuss them, or (7) revise the plan and present it to the board for further review and adoption.

• *Process improvement.* The group's purpose may be to identify and implement ways to improve productivity. The product is continuous improvement in measures of productivity. The process is a series of tasks aimed at outlining elements of the work process that is being improved, identifying frequent problems, determining the root causes of these problems, creating and trying ways to overcome these problems, and implementing solutions and measuring their effects.

• *Issue resolution.* The purpose could be to address and resolve a specific issue, for instance, finding ways to cut expenses, create new uses for a product, recruit and retain more members for an organization, or overcome disagreement and conflict about opposing points of view. The product is evidence that the issue has been resolved (for example, the budget has been cut by a desired amount or the desired number of new members have been recruited). The process is how the group goes about accomplishing these objectives. This might be discussions to define and clarify the problem, brainstorm ideas, evaluate those ideas, and vote on the ideas to select those to be presented as recommendations or actually begin work on implementing them.

• *Committee action.* The purpose of a committee may be to make something happen: hold an event, raise money, advertise, create a budget, or select a new employee, for example. The process depends on the action to be taken. Essentially the group must be clear about what is going to be done, why, how, where, and by whom. The leader, working jointly with the members of the group, outlines the elements of the task that they need to address, assigns roles or asks for volunteers, obtains resources, provides advice, and monitors progress.

Throughout this book, we will be discussing group leaders who confronted challenging and sometimes daunting tasks with little experience or guidance about what to do. The examples are from work and volunteer organizations. Sometimes we form groups for leisure activities. The outcomes are solely what we make of them.

Consider a group you are leading.

- Is it a committee, subcommittee, task force, club, board, or some other type of group?
- What are the key features of the group?
- What are the challenges?
- What does this mean for your role as leader?

Group Characteristics

To understand your leadership role, you need to know more about groups. Here, we explore characteristics of groups that determine what your group needs from you as their leader. Groups can vary in many ways. We look at ten major characteristics and then provide a tool for determining the characteristics of your group and how this can help you lead.

Purpose

What is the purpose for the group? Is it planning and running an event such as an annual meeting? Developing a new product or service or new use for an existing product or service? Designing and implementing a process such as performance appraisal? Determining ways to improve the quality of a product or process? Developing a new strategy such as new sales methods? Selecting personnel or deciding who gets a promotion or raise? Implementing a new data system? Formulating a vision and strategy? Resolving a conflict? The purpose has implications for the immediacy of the task, its importance to the organization and group members, and its difficulty.

Some tasks require merely following procedures that were designed previously, for example, repeating an annual event. The event is basically the same, but of course the group can be creative in making it better than ever before. Other group goals and tasks are totally open-ended with no precedent to follow and no right or best way to proceed. As a leader, you can involve members in discussing and determining group purpose and increase members' motivation and buy-in in the process.

Motivation or Reasons for Joining the Group

Why did the members join your group? How committed are they to it? Did they volunteer, or were they assigned? If they volunteered, do they care about the group's goals, or did they join just to socialize? If they were assigned, are they committed to the group's mission, or are they just going through the motions, participating because they have to? Do your members differ in their reasons for wanting to be part of the group? Some truly care about your group's goal. Others may want visibility for themselves, or they relish the challenge. Are your group's members motivated to work hard and treat their participation in the group seriously? As a leader, you can give the members time to express what they have to offer the group.

Number of Members

How large is the group? A committee may be just three people charged with a discrete task, for instance, come up with a new marketing strategy in three days. A task force may be ten to twenty people who represent diverse functions or fields in the organization. This group may be split into subgroups to accomplish different parts of the overall tasks. In general, the larger the group is, the more demands there are on the leader in all respects. For instance, if you are leading a large group, you will need to work hard to communicate clearly, get everyone to participate, overcome different vested interests, and foster member commitment and motivation. As a leader, you can consider the size of your group, its composition, and whether subgroups will be needed.

Member Diversity

The group is likely to vary in diversity in terms of ethnic or other demographic characteristics, as well as expertise and background. Generally diversity challenges the leader to make use of different skills and not let differences in approach, opinions, or biases get in the way. As the leader, you can foster members' identification with the group and overcome differences between members.

Member Turnover

What is the turnover in members of this group? Will the membership change over time or stay about the same, at least while the group is accomplishing a specific goal? Suppose people drop out. You will need to cope with losing their expertise and the feelings others may have about why they left. Did they leave because they were upset with you or other members? If you need new members, you will have to select, entice, and integrate newcomers into the group midstream.

Goal Clarity

What are your group's goals? Did you state them clearly? Do members share an understanding of what the group is trying to do? The clearer the goals are and the higher the agreement among members about the importance of achieving them, the easier the group's task will be. As a leader, be sure the group goals are clear.

Permanency and Time Frame

Is this group permanent or temporary? Permanent groups may have multiple tasks to perform over time, although the membership may change. A temporary group may have a single task to do and then disband. A related issue is how much time you have to complete the task. Is the group under a tight deadline? At what point in the process will you have to shift from a planning mode to a doing mode? As a leader, you will move the group from discussion to action.

Clarity of Work Process

Do members agree on the process the group will follow to accomplish its goals? Do they know what needs to be done by when? In other words, is the structure for the group's work laid out clearly when the group gets started, or does the group have to invent a process? This is a decision you make as the leader.

Your Role as Manager and Leader

Standard management tasks are organizing work, planning meetings, delegating tasks, monitoring progress, evaluating members' contributions to the group, giving members feedback about their performance, and monitoring the success of the group as a whole. As a manager, you exert control and manage the transactions. As a leader, you transform your members by engaging them in the group process. Rather than use control, you use influence. You collaborate with them to develop a clear mission and purpose for the group. You motivate your members to attend meetings and complete assignments outside meetings, facilitate the group process, empower them to make suggestions and take responsibility for the group's efforts, and generally shape and reshape the direction of the group in response to changing conditions. Most groups require both management and leadership, or what we refer to in Chapter Four as transactional and transformational leadership.

Your Power and Influence

Your power and influence as a leader may depend on whether you were appointed or elected. Some groups begin without a leader and then elect a leader from among the members. Such a leader would have the loyalty and trust of the group members as long as he or she behaves in a way that the members expect and want. Other times a person is the group leader because of organizational level, function, expertise, or assertiveness. For instance, the chief financial officer may chair the annual budget committee. This leader's power is vested in his or her position or knowledge. Other times, the leader may be appointed by a top executive because the executive has confidence in the leader. One of the leader's first tasks in such a case is to gain the trust of the group members by communicating clearly and meeting commitments. Even if you have the formal role as leader, you can share leadership with your members, empowering them to participate fully in the group process, shaping the group's goals, work methods, and products and representing the group to others. We will say more about shared leadership in Chapter Four.

Applying Group Characteristics

Now let's apply these characteristics to the group you are leading. For each of the following characteristics, circle the description that best applies to your group.

Purpose	Uncertain	Certain
Motivation	Low	High
Size	Large	Small
Diversity	Diverse	Homogeneous
Turnover	High	Low
Goal clarity	Ambiguous	Clear
Permanency or time frame	Limited time or tight deadline	Ongoing or no deadline
Process	Unstructured	Structured
Leader's role	Facilitating or Transforming	Controlling
Leader's power	Low	High

Count the number you circled on the left column of the characteristics. If the number is ten, you have your hands full: demands on the group and on you as the leader are likely to be high. Your responses might pinpoint areas that are likely to be problems or challenges, such as member turnover or low motivation, lack of clarity of purpose or process, or a tight deadline.

Cases

As examples, we examine the characteristics of two groups: a hospital quality improvement team and a product development team.

Example: Hospital Quality Improvement Team

This committee was established by the chief of medical services to improve emergency room operations. Team members were a nurse practitioner, a physician, a nurse, two lab technicians, and a systems trainer from the medical records office. The group's charge was to find a way to reduce the time it takes to obtain lab results in the emergency room. At the first meeting, the group elected the nurse practitioner as their leader. The nurse practitioner had worked in the emergency room for the last three years but had never led a quality improvement group.

Example: Product Development Team

This team was responsible for finding uses for a new technology. One team member was from the marketing department. There were two engineers, two people from manufacturing, one from product distribution, and another from sales. At the first meeting, the members suggested that the marketing department representative, who knew the customers and products well, chair the group.

The quality improvement team, led by the nurse practitioner, was established to improve emergency room operations. The product development team, led by the marketing department representative, was responsible for finding uses for a new technology (see Table 1.1 for a comparison of the groups).

**Table 1.1 Comparison of the Hospital Quality
Improvement Team and the Product Development Team**

Situation	Hospital Quality Improvement Team	Product Development Team
Purpose	Certain, but the goal was not specific: Reduce time needed to process lab reports and get the results to the emergency room.	Uncertain: Not clear what the product would be; the committee needed to investigate current products and capabilities, be creative about possible new products, explore possible markets, and determine production and distribution capabilities, to name a few of the needed tasks.
Motivation	Low: At least initially, it was not clear that the appointed members believed that the lab time could be reduced.	High: Members did not volunteer, but they had a vested interest in finding new products and improving the company's bottom line while contributing to their own employment security.
Size	Small.	Small.
Diversity	Diverse: All the needed functions were represented.	Diverse: All the needed functions were represented, but the group would have to reach outside to get information from others in the company as well as, and perhaps more important, from customers.
Turnover	Low—as long as the group made progress and people did not drop out.	Low—but more people may have been needed, or possibly the members of the team would need to change depending on the product the group began to develop and as the focus moved from design to implementation.

Situation	Hospital Quality Improvement Team	Product Development Team
Goal clarity	Ambiguous: Purpose was certain, but specifics about the goal—how much time to cut and how quickly to implement the change—were not.	Ambiguous: Saying that the company wanted a new product said nothing about what type of product it should be, whether it should address a new market or existing market, the cost of development, and so on.
Permanency and time frame	Limited duration: This was not meant to be a permanent group; there was no firm deadline either.	Limited duration: This group needed to get a new product started. It was unclear how long this should take; however, the powers that be would get impatient if the group did not come up with something promising within a reasonable period of time—one or two months, perhaps. Note that this group did not meet continuously but only several times a week; maybe they would find that they needed to meet more often.
Process	Structured (or at least, semi-structured): The group could follow some standard processes used by quality improvement teams, such as brainstorming ideas, collecting data about times for different lab tests, and experimenting with alternative procedures (see Chapter Six for a description of such procedures). The leader would need to learn these techniques from the hospital quality improvement professional staff to facilitate their use.	Unstructured: The group did not have standard procedures to follow; some members who had been on product development teams in the past may have had ideas about how to proceed.

(Continued)

**Table 1.1 Comparison of the Hospital Quality
Improvement Team and the Product Development Team, Continued**

Situation	Hospital Quality Improvement Team	Product Development Team
Leader's role	Influencing: Members needed to be convinced this was a worthwhile endeavor; each member had a different perspective coming from a different discipline.	Influencing: Although the leader was in charge, there were no set processes to follow and no one member had all the answers. All members would need to participate actively.
Leader's power	Low: As a nurse practitioner, the leader did not have the same authority as, say, the physician on the committee; however, the members knew that quality improvement teams in this hospital try to run in a way that all members of the group are treated, and treat each other, equally.	High: The leader could call the shots and was ultimately responsible for the outcome; however, the leader needed ideas and contributions from all group members.

The two cases were similar in degree of leader challenge. The main differences between the groups were that the quality improvement team had a more certain purpose, a lower member motivation, and lower leader power compared to the product development team.

Leaders' Comments

What did the leaders of these groups think about the challenges facing them? The nurse practitioner who led the quality improvement team said the following about the start of the process:

> I was very concerned that people on this group wouldn't listen to me. I thought that we could make a difference, but I was worried that the lab technicians would feel that we were telling them what to do. Actually, it occurred to us that improving time to get results may have less to do with processing specimens than getting them

from the emergency room to the lab and getting the results back. We needed some good information about how much time things take to convince the other members of the group that there was a real problem and that something could be done about it.

The leader of the product development team said at the start:

First of all, this was my first time leading a product development task force. What made things worse was that we didn't even know what kind of product we should develop. Of course, we reasoned that probably the product should be related to something we manufactured and sold already, but also we recognized that it could be something totally different. We were going to have to think out of the box and stay focused on getting something done. I could see us spinning our wheels in never-ending discussions and not making any decisions. I felt good that we had some strong people on the team who knew our customers and understood sales and marketing. They should have good ideas about how to get into new lines of businesses. It was exciting. This could really make a big difference to our business if we came up with the right idea. It was a big IF, though.

Determine How Closely Members Need to Work Together

Within each of the different types of short-term groups, members may need to work together to different degrees.

Groups in Which Each Member Has a Separate Task

In some groups, the members work independently at first. They bring their work back to a central group and present it. The group might vote on decisions based on the information brought back by individuals. The members do not necessarily bounce their ideas off one another or work together to come up with solutions. They might each have totally different abilities and responsibilities to the group as a whole. In other groups, members depend on each other to do the group's work.

Interdependence in Action

In athletics, all team members work together to win the game against their opponent. They pass the ball, run next to their team-mates, cheer them on from the sidelines, allow a teammate to make a goal by passing the ball, and so on. In music, duo piano players are careful not to bump their partner's hand as they cross over to catch the next note on the keyboard. In orchestras, the violins play more quietly during the cello aria. Similarly, in work groups, the commit-tee members may work together to produce their final report. Even if they do not totally agree on all issues, they come to consensus for the good of the group. All members contribute to the slide presenta-tion that will be given by the leader to company executives, and the leader will give all members credit for participating in the work.

As an example, suppose an artist, designer, architect, contrac-tor, banker, and developer form a group to design and build a new shopping center. They share a common goal but need each other's expertise to get the job done. They need to meet regarding the specifications of the shopping center, and then they may work alone and report back to the group about their progress. They may work in parallel. They each come up with an idea and bring their idea to the group. The group votes on which idea to choose. Then each member uses his or her expertise to develop part of the project. They meet again to show each other what they have. If they work as a team, they might brainstorm during one meeting and develop what the end result will look like. Then they will discuss how each can use his or her own expertise to contribute to the project. They might communicate between meetings, send each other ideas, or bounce ideas off one another. The leader provides feedback and keeps the group on task.

We can also talk about relationships between groups, for instance, several groups working together or in tandem. There are groups that work toward a common goal but do not actually work together. Consider religious groups: they may have common beliefs and raise money for similar causes, but the groups never actually meet, except perhaps at large annual conferences. Or a company's CEO may form different groups to work on the same product: for example, regional sales teams working to increase the company's sales overall, with each team taking actions that fit the competitive conditions in their region.

Summary

This chapter reviewed different types of groups (committees, subcommittees, task forces, project teams, clubs, boards, and councils) and the challenges they present to a leader, including the extent to which members need to work closely together to accomplish the group's mission.

- The type of group you are leading determines the challenges you will face. A committee that is short term and task specific needs to make progress quickly. A task force that is long term and requires information from different functions needs considerable coordination. This type of group benefits from frequent and open communication, member participation in establishing group goals and work methods, and coordination to be sure the members integrate their different functions. A board that provides oversight of functions carried out by others has to collect information and track progress of the individuals and groups under their jurisdiction. A club that has a social agenda as its primary focus (even though it may do other things) needs members' active involvement and participation to be sure the group is meeting their needs.

- Groups differ in their purpose, members' motivation, task and organizational structure, and the way the leader is chosen. The purpose may be to create a vision or strategy, improve a work process, resolve an issue, or plan and implement an action or event. The purpose and intended product guide the process that the leader and group adopt. External factors, such as deadlines, resources, and expectations, pose challenges for the leader and the group and determine what they do, how they do it, and how fast they work.

- Group characteristics are purpose, motivation, size, diversity, turnover, goal clarity, permanence, well-defined process, the leader's role in influencing or controlling, and the leader's power and command of resources. Assess the leader's role and the group on each of these characteristics to determine the degree of difficulty the group leader is likely to encounter and plan the leadership strategy.

Chapter 2

SETTING THE GROUNDWORK FOR A HIGH-PERFORMING TEAM

You might ask yourself, How do I know if I have the right people in my group? How do I determine how much time is needed for us to get our work done? Suppose I underestimate this? Suppose none of my group members have had any experience working on this type of task before? Suppose we do not understand what we are supposed to do or what higher leadership wants from us?

This chapter describes how to make your group into a team—that is, a group in which members are interdependent, cooperative, responsible, honest, and productive. There are three keys to creating a high-performing team: (1) be sure you have the right talent and motivated members, (2) be sure your members have the time to participate and the group has time to get the work done, and (3) be sure the group members are clear about the task. The chapter shows you how to evaluate whether your committee or task force has these critical factors and how you can make sure they are present.

After reading this chapter, you will be able to:

- Describe the three elements of a high-performing team.
- Choose group members who have the abilities and experience your group needs to accomplish its goals.
- Develop a shared vision and establish rules for how members will work together.
- Use different decision-making methods, such as consensus, fist-to-five consensus building, traditional majority, absolute majority, minority vote, and multivoting.

- Know how to avoid groupthink.
- Structure the group's task so that members are clear about what they have to do.
- Determine whether group members have the time to devote to the group's work.
- Establish methods to evaluate the group's results.
- Diagnose your group's potential to become a high-performing team.
- Use member diversity as an advantage, not a source of dysfunction.

Qualities of a High-Performing Team

Now that you have a good understanding of characteristics of small groups and developmental stages from the first three chapter, you might reasonably wonder what you need to do to be sure you are successful. In this chapter, we get down to brass tacks: what it takes to create a high-performing group. Three elements are critical:

Talent: Group members have the capabilities and motivation.

Time: Deadlines are met.

Task: Objectives, methods, and assessment methods are clear.

Differences Between High- and Low-Performing Groups

Two researchers at Cornell University, Jeff Ericksen and Lee Dyer (2004), collected data from six project groups, ranging in size from five to nine members, using interviews, observations, documents, and surveys. The group tasks were varied: deciding on the acquisition of another firm, developing a new business-to-consumer Web site, designing two e-commerce pilot programs, developing a new business model to boost sales of a new product, developing a new global service solution, and designing a strategy for delivering distance learning. Project performance was measured by adherence to deadlines, quality of products or solutions, and degree of group ownership of products or solutions.

Ericksen and Dyer used these measures of performance to identify the groups as high performing or low performing. They discovered that the high-performing groups differed from the low-performing groups in how they were mobilized and launched. At the outset, all six project groups received small amounts of background information, general descriptions of their projects and expected outcomes, and deadlines. However, the leaders of the high- and low-performing groups used very different approaches to mobilization and launching the groups. Getting started on the right foot made all the difference to their later success.

In particular, the leaders of the groups that turned out to be high performing created favorable initial conditions. They ensured that the groups had ample time, suitable talent, and clear and compelling tasks. This propelled them forward. In contrast, members of the groups that turned out to be low performing felt there was inadequate time, they lacked the capabilities they needed to do the job, and they were not sure what they were trying to accomplish. They also felt that the work had low priority to the organization and the deadlines were not serious, so they failed to meet time lines. The leaders of the low-performing groups had overlooked members' task-relevant knowledge and skills and time commitments when they invited people to join the group. In contrast, the high-performing groups used launch meetings to agree on operational tasks, addressing specifically what they needed to accomplish and how it could be done. The members had a clear sense of the problems they faced and ways to solve them. This stimulated short-term action and facilitated learning so the group could face later problems and barriers head on.

In high-performing groups, members have the expertise needed to help the group and a sense of ownership for whatever the group is doing. They care about what the group is trying to accomplish, and they want to do a good job (Hackman, 2002). Often members are recruited because of their title (for example, they are all heads of a department). This does not ensure that they have buy-in to the task at hand or that they have the skills to achieve the task, however. Leaders need to establish member buy-in during the early stages of the group. If members help to develop the idea and set the vision, they are likely to feel committed to it. If they have not had a chance to shape the vision, they may wonder if it is worth their time.

In addition to technical knowledge, skills, and abilities, group members need the skills to work together effectively. That is, they need integration skills (West, 2002):

- Skill to resolve conflict: the ability to recognize and encourage desirable conflict, for instance, examining different sides to an issue and discouraging undesirable conflict, for instance, name-calling
- Skill to use win-win negotiation strategies: the ability to distinguish between, and encourage or discourage, task-related conflict and interpersonal conflict
- Collaborative problem-solving skill: the ability to identify situations requiring participative group problem solving
- Skill to use decentralized communication networks to improve communication
- Skill to communicate openly and supportively
- Skill to integrate and focus group members: use of goal setting and performance management; monitoring and providing feedback to individuals and the group; and coordinating and synchronizing activities, information, and tasks

These integration skills lead members to work collaboratively, making the group more innovative and effective. The group members use these integration skills to develop a shared vision and establish how they will make decisions.

Developing a Shared Vision

A shared vision is a common view of the group, its purpose, its membership, and the work that needs to get done. Here are some techniques you might try in order to understand your group and help your group develop a shared vision:

1. Hold a group discussion about the purpose for the group. Use a flip chart or computer to list the major goals as you see them. Ask the group for clarification. Also, discuss the importance and urgency of the group's work. Do your members agree on these? If not, address why not. Do they believe the goal is under their control? Do they believe they can accomplish it? Discuss why it is important to work in a group rather than individually—for instance, because there is a need for coordination, creativity, diverse knowledge and expertise, or working across functions. You can build individual motivation and enthusiasm for the group's goal by emphasizing the unique potential contributions of each group member.

2. Identify the possible different perspectives about the group's vision (purpose and process). Do the exercise in technique 1 individually at first, and then have the members talk about their views of the group's goals, characteristics, and methods. For instance, you could ask each member to draft a vision statement of the group's purpose. Then go around the group and read them aloud. Record the major points on a flip chart. Next, split the group in two, and ask each subgroup to revise the statement. Again, read and record the central elements of each. Now have the group as a whole revise and develop one statement.

3. Remind members who the sponsors are for the group (executives, board of directors, one or more managers) and the

sponsors' roles (to advise, track, assess). How often does the group have to report to the sponsor? List the stakeholders: others who care about the group outcomes. How will they influence the group? What do they expect from the group? Are these expectations different from those of the sponsors? If so, how can you resolve these differences, or at least recognize that these differences exist? Establish the stake the group members have in achieving the group's goals.

4. Ask the group to list the key characteristics of the group that may affect its performance (diversity, commitment, need for coordination). For each, indicate whether it is likely to facilitate performance or be a barrier that you need to overcome.

5. List the challenges your group faces—for instance, doing something no one else in the group has done before (ambiguous, uncertain, few if any models to follow—paving new ground), complexity (multiple elements, need for coordination), or resource requirements (time, money, facilities).

6. List the work methods, that is, the sorts of things your group will be doing—for instance, planning, generating ideas, voting, making decisions. Talk about the extent to which the group members are dependent on each other to do the work.

7. Talk about rules for group operation. List everyone's ideas for rules. Ask the group to prioritize them. For the top three or four, ask if everyone can abide by them, and if not, to speak up now. Examples of rules might be, "No one comes to a meeting late," "No one will make a commitment to do something they know in advance they can't do," "We will respect each other, for instance, listen when someone is talking," or "We will make decisions by making motions, discussing them, and voting."

8. Establish a rough time line, and discuss whether the time line is realistic. Since groups tend to underestimate the time needed to complete a task, identify factors that might prevent the group from completing its work on time. Talk about whether these can be avoided. If not, adjust your time line.

9. Discuss what you expect from the members, including the roles you expect them to play. Be specific. This may include giving you advice about leading the group and the direction the group is taking. It may include being a facilitator, helping to evaluate the group process, and suggesting ways the group can do better.

10. Discuss how the group members feel about the group. Are they here voluntarily and looking forward to participating eagerly, or are they here involuntarily and wish they were somewhere else? Chances are most members feel the same way. If they are not looking forward to the group task, ask them what they might do to improve the situation, whether it be make the best of it or turn it around to be a worthwhile experience. If they are looking forward to it, agree that they will let you know if they begin to feel otherwise. You want to maintain morale and nip problems in the bud.

Deciding How to Decide

When you and your group members formulate ground rules for working together, you can establish how you will make decisions. For instance, you might agree that any decision involving a commitment of funds requires a two-thirds majority. This might be spelled out in the organization's constitution, or it might be decided by the group at the first meeting or even when the need to make the decision arises. If you do not determine how you will make decisions when the group begins but wait until you have a need to make a decision, then the decision process may itself be fraught with politics and confusion. For instance, if you are about to make an important decision, a few people who have a minority opinion may call for a two-thirds majority vote, knowing (or believing) that a majority cannot be achieved. In general, the best policy is to review decision-making methods and alternatives early—even during the first meeting or as part of the group's constitution. Consider the following decision-making methods.

Consensus

In consensus decision making, all members participate as much as possible (Niziol & Free, 2005). The goal is for the group to arrive at a decision that every member can accept and support. This may not be the favored outcome of each member, but each person can accept it. The group reaches consensus when each member has reached this point, and so there is 100 percent buy-in. The steps to reaching consensus include (1) clarifying and discussing the topic, (2) periodically testing for consensus (seeing whether each member can live with the decision), (3) allowing enough time for active discussion and participation by everyone, and (4) giving feedback about what you hear and the extent to which the group members are willing to live with a particular alternative. Ask members to express their agreement by a show of hands. The advantage of this method is that everyone gets to express an opinion, and unlike voting, it does not create winners and losers. The disadvantage is that it takes time.

Use the fist-to-five consensus-building method when group members must be committed to the decision and contribute to its implementation in some way. This technique is used in groups to assess the agreement with and opposition to an issue. Members raise their fingers to indicate their extent of agreement or opposition using the fingers of one hand as a five-point rating scale (Fletcher, 2002). If they hold up fewer than three fingers, give them a chance to voice their opinion. One finger means, "I still need to discuss certain issues and suggest changes that should be made." Two means, "I am more comfortable with the proposal but would like to discuss some minor issues." Three means, "I'm not in total agreement, but feel comfortable to let this decision or proposal pass without further discussion." Four means, "I think it is a good idea [or decision] and will work for it." Five means, "It's a great idea, and I will be one of the leaders in implanting it." (The fist, of course, means no agreement.) The advantage of this method is that members show each other where they stand on an issue as it is evolving. The disadvantage is that it takes time. Use this method when various degrees of buy-in are okay—that is, all members do not have to be totally committed to the decision but giving everyone a chance to express their views and conclusion is important for members to remain committed to the group.

Majority Rule Voting

Majority rule can happen in three ways: traditional majority, absolute majority, and supermajority.

Traditional Majority. A motion is made and seconded, the floor is open for discussion, and then the leader or another member calls for a vote. The alternative with the most votes wins. Abstentions may be allowed. The advantage of this method is that it is fast. The disadvantage is that some members will not be satisfied with the outcome, which may lessen their commitment to the group as well as the specific decision. If members feel they lose to the majority every time, they will become disenfranchised and may withdraw their support or even stop coming to meetings.

Absolute Majority. Compared to a more traditional majority vote, the concept of an absolute majority is a more thorough and comprehensive way of reaching group consensus. In this scenario, the passing of a vote requires that all members of the group vote, including those who are usually not present and not voting (Absolute majority, 2006). More than half of the members of the group, including those absent who must be contacted, must vote in favor of a proposition in order for it to be passed. The advantage of this method is that it calls on everyone to participate and therefore emphasizes the importance of the issue and asking everyone to contribute to make the decision. The disadvantage is that some members who are on the periphery of the group may not fully understand the issue or may not want to have a vote. Also, getting all the members to a meeting for the vote may be difficult. Use this method when you want to call attention to the importance of an issue.

Supermajority.   A supermajority requires that for a proposal or candidate to pass, it must gain a specified level of support that exceeds a simple majority. A two-thirds majority is common. This vote means that the vote for a proposal or candidate must equal or exceed twice the number of votes against it. This actually protects the interests of the minority. The higher the percentage required for a proposal to pass, the smaller the minority to which control passes (Supermajority, 2006). That is, it could take only one-third of the group to be opposed to a proposal for it to fail under a two-thirds majority rule. The advantage of this method is that serious issues are not passed unless most of the members agree. The disadvantage is that a majority may be hard to achieve, thereby slowing or halting the group's ability to move ahead. Use this method for important issues when it is okay if not everyone is in favor of it.

Multivoting

This is a way to identify alternatives that are important to a group. After brainstorming a list of issues or ideas, this method determines which alternatives to address first. Divide the total number of items by three, and this becomes the number of votes each person has to distribute. Ask each member to place this number of votes beside the items, allowing more than one vote per item but no more than the total number that each person can distribute. The advantage of this method is that it is a fast way to reduce and prioritize a large number of alternatives and have everyone participate in the process. The disadvantage is that each issue or idea is not discussed separately and those not making the cut may be dismissed without additional consideration, although the group can return to them later. Use this method as a preliminary decision making tool to set priorities for action.

Avoiding Groupthink

A shared vision is one thing; groupthink is another. Groupthink is faulty decision making. It happens when group members always want to be in agreement and members openly agree with a perceived group position even if individual group members privately disagree. An exaggerated desire to go along with the perceived group position, it happens when members see themselves as highly cohesive and part of a special, distinctive group and as doing important work for a common goal. They feel they are in an in-group, a clique if you will, that becomes more important than saying anything that may disrupt people's feelings of belonging.

The concept of groupthink was conceptualized by Irving L. Janis (1972) at Yale University. It is caused by high levels of cohesiveness, structural defects in the group (such as insulation, lack of leader impartiality, lack of procedural norms, and member homogeneity), and provocative situational contexts such as low group efficacy and high stress (Henningsen, Henningsen, Eden, & Cruz, 2006). Groupthink leads to rationalizations, pressures to conform, biased perceptions of out-group members, self-censorship, and illusions of the group's invulnerability, morality, and unanimity. The result is pressure to go along with the favored group position. This leads to defects in decision making, such as an incomplete survey of objectives, failure to examine risks associated with the preferred choice, poor information searches, selective bias in processing information, failure to reappraise alternatives, and failure to provide contingency plans—in a nutshell, not processing information effectively. Nevertheless, some people are likely to resist groupthink. In particular, group members who have high confidence in their opinions and viewpoints about alternatives are less likely to feel pressure to go along with the group.

To avoid groupthink, consider all members' views before making decisions. Bring in outside experts, and research how similar decisions have worked out in different organizations. You might revisit decisions in the light of new research or invite new members to join the group as a way of encouraging fresh ideas. Encourage all members to speak up, and avoid squelching members who express outlying or unusual ideas.

Benefits of a High-Performing Team

In high-performing teams, members are attuned to the time frame that they set for themselves or is imposed by others. They plan their tasks and track their progress with the deadline in mind. If they get bogged down despite good intentions, which is fairly common, they may need to regroup and change their work methods, assignments, or even product design in order to meet the deadline.

Regarding task, effective groups have clear objectives, methods, and assessments as early as possible in the group process. Members have a common understanding of what they are trying to do. They also agree on the methods they will use to accomplish their objectives. This may take a good deal of discussion and debate, but ultimately they agree on what needs to be done, how they will do it, who will do it, and by when. Then the group needs to have clear methods for assessing their progress, such as deadlines for different elements of the task and whether the objectives have been met.

For example, consider a committee of staff and patrons in a small public library to develop a plan for increased access to electronic library services. Objectives might be to (1) evaluate the library's current electronic holdings, computers in the library, and accessibility of the library's Web site and electronic holdings for patrons working at home or in their businesses; (2) collect information about what other similar libraries are doing in this area; (3) determine patrons' usage and needs to evaluate the gap in services; (4) recommend expansion of services (for example, adding computers, improving the library's server, redoing the Web site to make it more user friendly, purchasing or leasing online databases); (5) establish costs and priorities and suggest time lines for implementation; and (6) consider current costs that might be cut in order to hold down the additional cost of their recommendations.

The committee needs to achieve these objectives within the next three months, two months before the community will vote on the library budget, giving the library board time to review and fine-tune the recommendations and incorporate them into the proposed budget. The committee recognizes the immediacy of their work and knows that not having a solid plan before the vote would mean putting off any expansion for another year, which would severely limit patron services given the increased importance of electronic reference material. So the committee may agree on meeting weekly during the first six weeks and twice weekly during the next six weeks. They will examine data on usage, develop and administer a patron survey about needs, analyze patrons' requests and librarians' perceptions of need, and explore alternative computer configurations and database costs, including planning for increases in the costs of currently used electronic media. In order to track progress, the committee may establish time lines for completing the different objectives. They may need to reevaluate their work plan as the process unfolds. The committee members may disagree initially about how to survey patrons or find that developing the questionnaire or interview questions is taking more time than initially anticipated. They might get bogged down hearing the spiel of a computer salesperson who has a proposal to increase the number of computers in the library. They may be influenced by politically active community members who are lobbying for cutting the library's budget. These events and occurrences may change the committee's game plan, but the members will make these adjustments recognizing their objectives, time line, and the library board's and director's expectations.

In general, high-performing groups generate high-quality outputs, whether they are formulating a plan, making recommendations, or implementing a program. The group members agree on their vision for what they are trying to accomplish.

In high-performing groups, members are in sync. An example from the world of music is when wonderful coloratura soprano auditions for a choir. She sings a glorious aria, yet the conductor does not choose her for the group. The conductor recognizes her talent and abilities but also fears that she might out-sing the other sopranos—essentially that she will not be a group player. The group will sound like backup singers following an opera star rather than an ensemble. The star must put aside her solo talent and listen intently to the other singers in order to enhance the group effort. This happens in work groups as well. If one member is interested only in getting the attention of the boss at the expense of other group members, a coordinated effort will not result. The benefit of a group is to hear all of its members. All need to be engaged in the same effort, creating a greater resource of abilities, time, materials, and production—more like an orchestra than a soloist.

High-performing groups know their audience. When a group is preparing a presentation, the members must consider whether the audience will be a small group of higher-level executives or a large group of peers. Perhaps a slide presentation is appropriate in some situations, but hard copies of charts, maps, and large visuals are appropriate in others. Some goals require that data be presented; others call for a diagram or chart. Informality is appropriate in some settings, while formal, serious speaking is a must in others.

The Challenge of Creating a High-Performing Team

The three main components of a high-performing team (talent, time, and task) pose three clear guidelines. You might think of them as challenges:

1. Be sure the group has talented members (those with the skills, knowledge, and background) to do the job.

2. Be sure that the members have the time to spend on the task. If they are too busy doing other things or if other things are more important to them, chances are that they will not be effective group members. Also, be sure that group members

understand that they must devote sufficient time to work together—that meetings will be at mutually convenient times and that members schedule time to work on the group's task outside meetings. Although you cannot make them have time or do the work, you *can* be clear that this is your expectation.

3. Be sure that the task itself is clear and significant (something the members understand and think of as worthwhile for the organization and themselves) and that work methods and assignments are clear and can be accomplished in the time allowed. Also, be sure there is a way to evaluate the quality of the group's product. Establish assessment methods at the outset so members are clear about how you and others will evaluate the group's product.

When leaders realize that the task is important, they are likely to select members with the needed talent and time and structure the task to meet deadlines, produce a high-quality result, and foster a sense of membership and ownership of the group process and outcome.

Recognizing a High-Performing Group

Do you know a high-performing group when you see one? Think about a group that you have been part of in the past as a member or the leader. If you would say that the group was a high-performing group, identify in which ways it was so:

1. Did group members have the skills, knowledge, and abilities needed for the work of the group?   Yes   No

2. Were the members clear about the group's goals from the start?   Yes   No

3. Did members feel the group's task was important?   Yes   No

4. Did the members have a clear picture from the start of what the group was trying to accomplish?   Yes   No

5. Did members get to know each other well enough early on so that they know how each person could contribute to the group?	Yes	No
6. Did members have the time they needed to work on the task?	Yes	No
7. Did members have a clear idea about their roles, that is, who does what when?	Yes	No
8. Did the group meet deadlines?	Yes	No
9. Did the group accomplish its goals?	Yes	No
10. Were members proud of the group's product?	Yes	No

If you answered yes to all ten questions, then this group was indeed high performing. If you answered no to one or more questions, what were the impediments to the group's functioning and outcomes? How did the group overcome them? Did the problems arise because of inadequate talent, time, or task clarity? If these factors were present at the outset, did having them help the group overcome impediments? For instance, if clients changed their expectations (set higher goals or changed what they wanted from the group), did the leader and the group seek new members with different skills, revise the time lines, or redefine the components of the task and their vision of the outcome? If they were not clear about these components to begin with, chances are they will be further mired in doubt and confusion when the situation changes.

Assessing Your Group's Potential for High Performance

Low-performing groups lack members with the skills, talent, or motivation to work together. The group is without a clear sense of purpose, and members do not know what to do when. They are confused and inactive. As a result, the group misses deadlines and produces products or services that do not meet your expectations or those of the clients who will use the products or services. Of course, many groups struggle at various points along the way, even high-performing groups. The difference is that the high-performing group is able to overcome barriers.

Your role as leader is to be a champion for the project and group. Stack the deck by creating conditions that foster high performance. If the current members lack the talent or motivation, find new members who do if this is possible (it may not be). If members lack the time they need to work on the group project, speak to the members' supervisors and try to free up their time. Of course, people have to be motivated enough to go beyond the regular workday and meet and work after hours. Set milestones to help members track the group's progress. Pace the group's tasks by determining how much time is likely to be needed for various tasks, and set a schedule for completing different elements of the task. If clients' expectations or definitions of high-quality outputs are not clear, help clarify them, perhaps inviting clients to group meetings to express and discuss their expectations. If the group is slowing down and in danger of missing important deadlines, change the task or ask for more time. You can also change the direction of group discussions from a brainstorming mode to a doing mode.

Many times group members do not have the skills they need. You can help them acquire these by finding resources for training and development—for instance, journal clubs in which group members read and discuss what they need to know to be more effective.

In empowered groups, members have the ability to make decisions, are accountable for the outcomes of their decisions, accept responsibility for these outcomes, and can solve problems on their own. They feel competent to perform tasks well, are free to choose how to carry out these tasks, believe their work is meaningful, and think their work has a positive effect on their organization. A study of 453 members of 121 service technician groups found that the more members felt empowered, the more they believed that their group process was positive, that is, that they were able to plan, conduct their work, and resolve conflicts well (Mathieu, Gilson, & Ruddy, 2006). The better their group process was, the more their customers were satisfied. Empowerment is a result of what you do as a leader, the training that is available to help members carry out their work, the organizational support such as resources and time, and the extent to which the group's goals are clear and structured (because the group members impose the structure themselves or because the task has specific things that need to be done).

Do the members of your group *feel* empowered? Do they share a collective sense that they have the responsibility and the authority to control their work? Do they believe that the work of the group is meaningful? Here are some items you can use to rate empowerment in your group. (We adapted these items from Matheiu et al., 2006.) Use a five-point scale from 1 = low to 5 = high:

Authority

_____ My group is empowered to change our work processes in order to improve.

_____ We can solve problems on our own.

_____ We are free to choose how to carry out our work.

Responsibility

_____ Members of my group are responsible for determining the best way to meet the expectations others have of us.

_____ We are accountable for the outcomes of our decisions.

_____ People will blame us if something goes wrong.

_____ People will give us the credit if they like what our group does.

Significance of the Work

_____ Our group's work is important.

_____   Our group members care about the quality of our work.

_____   Others outside the group have high expectations for us.

_____   What we do as a group matters to the larger organization.

Now that you know the elements of a high-performing team, let's look at what you need to do to make it happen.

Diversity and Group Process

Having the right mix of people—the right skills and backgrounds—is important to high performance. Group diversity is a mixed blessing. You want group members who bring the different areas of knowledge, skills, experiences, and viewpoints to the group's work. Nevertheless, diversity may add leadership challenges such as poor communication and conflicts. The key is managing diversity to ensure that the group members recognize, value, and use the unique contributions of each member. The leader of a diverse group needs to promote information exchange among the group members. Members may fear being rejected by other group members and may refrain from openly sharing ideas. Therefore, leaders must create work environments that encourage dialogue and in which members can learn from others and about themselves (Drach-Zahavy & Somech, 2001). Diversity of expertise and demographic characteristics such as gender can be important to group outcomes.

Group Composition Affects Group Process

Group composition and context determine what the group does. Group process, in turn, affects outputs such as innovativeness and effectiveness. Michael West (1996) studied top management groups in twenty-seven hospitals in Great Britain. He defined innovativeness in terms of the degree to which the ideas and products the group generates are novel or even radical and how many ideas are generated. He also measured group effectiveness. In particular, he explored whether group composition (such factors as group size, diversity of knowledge of group members), organizational context (resources and support for teamwork), and group processes (clear objectives, active member participation, and encouragement of innovation) affected innovativeness and effectiveness. He discovered that group processes were more highly related to innovativeness than group composition or context. However, having more innovative group members increased the extent to which the group came up with radical innovations. West also showed that groups in which members had a diversity of knowledge and skills were likely to be more innovative as long as they integrated these competencies with the group process. Moreover, creativity occurred mainly during the early stages of group processes. In addition, creativity decreased when there were high levels of demands and potential threats for not succeeding at implementation.

As a leader, be aware of situational conditions and demands that may limit your group members' ability to take advantage of the diversity of skills, knowledge, and talents. You may or may not control who is in your group and the resources you have available. More than likely, you do control the group's process and can work to clarify objectives, provide opportunities for members to participate, and reinforce members' innovative ideas.

Does Having More Women Help a Group?

A study that explored gender diversity in groups that are usually mostly male found that more women in the group improved the group's confidence in itself early on, which helped the group become more cohesive, work together more effectively, and perform better, especially on a cognitive problem-solving task.

Researchers from the U.S. Air Force and several universities studied participants in the five-week U.S. Air Force officer development program, geared to developing officers' teamwork (Hirschfeld, Jordan, Field, Giles, & Armenakis, 2005). Ninety-two groups of participants engaged in three tasks that required them to learn objectives and rules, formulate a strategy, organize their resources, develop plans for execution, assess progress during implementation, and take any needed corrective actions. Two of the tasks required field operations that entailed physical performance. Another task was problem solving and required mental performance and verbal communication. All three tasks required group members' interdependence. That is, group members needed to work together to do well. Groups also competed against each other, which added an incentive for cooperation. An officer who did not participate observed each group throughout the five weeks. Groups ranged in size from eleven to thirteen members. There were one to four women per group, with an average of two. The average age of all participants was thirty-one. Group confidence was measured by a survey during the first week of the program after they had participated in a team-building exercise but before they had begun any of the tasks. During the last week of the program, participants completed a survey measuring social cohesion (team unity, trust, spirit, and cooperative communication), and the observer rated the teamwork of his or her group.

The results showed that more women within groups contributed to better group problem solving but slightly worse group results on physically demanding tasks. Groups' higher early confidence was related to doing better on the tasks early on and having social cohesion later. Early group self-confidence helped the groups get off to a strong start in performing better and developing teamwork. The researchers suggested that a higher proportion of women in a group may be most beneficial when organizations' formal cultures and policies strongly promote the full inclusion of women (gender equality).

> This study has implications for organizations in which high-status roles in groups are usually occupied by men. As a leader, consider that groups with more female representation may engage in better problem solving. Also, be sure that gender stereotypes do not influence how members treat each other. Include all members fully in the group process.

Effects of Diversity on Group Decision Making

Diversity should enhance generating ideas and increase the range of opinions in evaluating those ideas. However, it may cause conflict in making a final decision unless the group is committed to a common goal.

Think about how diversity may have an effect on a group depending on what the group is doing. Suppose your group is going through a decision-making process that requires you and your members to generate ideas (brainstorm), then evaluate those ideas, and ultimately make a choice. As the group proffers ideas, diversity of opinion, background, and experience should result in a wide range of ideas—more than would occur without the diversity. When the group discusses the ideas, the group members' different vantage points should give rise to differences in opinion. If you encourage open expression of opinions, your members' vested interests will be evident. Still, the diversity should make for a constructive and broad discussion and give your members ideas to think about that they would not have considered on their own. When the group makes the final decision, the degree of dissension among the members may lead to arguments and disgruntlement unless the members feel that the group has a common goal that supersedes their individual interests. Leaders need to encourage members' participation as a way to increase their identification with the group and their commitment to a shared goal. Then everyone (or most members) will base the final decision on what is in the group's best interest.

Managing Diversity

Most of us presume that diverse groups are more creative and perform better than homogeneous groups because they bring together people with different viewpoints and backgrounds and have access to a variety of resources—the knowledge, skills, information, expertise, and networks that each member brings to the group. However, we also presume that members of diverse groups may have trouble getting along and that conflict, or at least miscommunication, is inevitable. People prefer to work with others who are similar to them rather than different. Members of homogeneous groups feel that the group is more cohesive right from the start.

Elizabeth Mannix of Cornell University and Margaret A. Neale of Stanford University reviewed the research on diverse groups and discovered several conditions that determine whether diversity has a positive or negative effect on group performance (Mannix & Neale, 2005). Fortunately, group leaders can influence these conditions, exploiting the advantages and avoiding the disadvantages of diverse groups. To be more specific, some types of diversity are more likely to have positive effects than others without any intervention. Demographic diversity (for instance, diversity of race, gender, and age) is more likely to have negative effects. National diversity may cause members to put each other into social categories, at least until they begin to recognize the value of the different perspectives the members bring to the group (Dahlin, Weingart, & Hinds, 2006). Other types of diversity, for instance, diversity of functional expertise and personality, are more likely to have positive effects. Having group members with different educational backgrounds (for instance, different college majors) is likely to have a positive influence on the range and depth of information used by the group, although it might make integrating the information difficult, especially if the group is particularly diverse. Another way to think of diversity is the range of experiences that each person brings to the group—essentially, diversity within members as well as between members. When group members have a variety of functional backgrounds, they are more likely to share their knowledge and experiences with the group (Bunderson & Sutcliffe, 2002). So having groups in which members differ from one another *and* each brings a wide range of functional backgrounds can increase group effectiveness.

In order to overcome the potential negative effects of diversity and take advantage of the positive effects, you will have to do more than work on improving group process skills, such as conflict management, communication, and decision making. In particular, Mannix and Neale (2005) recommend the following:

Be sure that minority opinions are heard. Group members who have different perspectives should feel free to express their viewpoints. In general, create an environment in the group that encourages and rewards learning and change for all members. Show the group members that you value each person's individual identity and outlook. Connect the group's diversity to the task, and ask members to apply their different perspectives and views to the group's vision and strategy. When members are open to learning as a goal, they welcome the possibility of change. The group leader should be explicit about valuing the variety of opinions and insights represented in the group and recognize that it will not be easy for the group members to express their diverse opinions. (See Chapter Seven for more about how to create a learning environment, particularly one that supports learning about and applying new information and ideas, even in a short-term group.)

Determine whether the task requires diverse group members. Mannix and Neale (2005) found that the value of group diversity depends on the group's task. Diverse groups are especially important for tasks that require innovation and exploration of new opportunities. In such cases, members start with differing knowledge and perspectives, and they learn together to develop their own, new common understanding. Homogeneous groups are probably better for tasks that exploit and implement the facts and opinions that people hold already since there is no new learning and there will be little disagreement.

Build bridges that connect members. Emphasize what members have in common rather than their differences. Help the group develop a shared goal and common identity that rises above the identities of individual members or subgroups. In other words, create a feeling of "we" by emphasizing the common goals that all the group members want to achieve and that "each of us will succeed if the group succeeds." When group members feel they are working toward a common goal, they are likely to have constructive (task-focused) conflicts and less likely to have destructive (relationship-focused) conflicts. Demographically diverse groups that share a common group or organizational culture are more likely to interact, cooperate, and generate new ideas than those in a culture that is individualistic in which members do not share a common identity or in which they tend to be biased.

Exercises for Creating a High-Performing Team

Here are several exercises to help you make your group into a high-performing team by focusing on talent, time, and task.

Talent: List the elements of the task that you perceive. Indicate the expertise required for each point. List who on the committee has that expertise. Are you relying on one or two people to do too many things? Do you need more people with similar expertise? Do you need people with different expertise? List who might be available. Does the group have sufficient diversity of skills and knowledge to do the job? If so, point out the group's diversity as one of its strengths so the members are well aware of the contributions each is expected to make to the group effort and that you value each person.

Time: Do members have the necessary time to devote to the group? Is the time frame for the group to accomplish the goal realistic? Collect calendars of availability from each person. To the extent possible, know who will be away or busy with other work at different times during the expected duration of the committee's work.

Task: Consider what you would do if you do not have the option of selecting group members and do not have the expertise you believe will be needed. This is when task structure and timing are particularly critical. This is also when group turnover or group development and education may be useful. Have each member list the components of the task—what needs to be done. Compare lists to generate a comprehensive list. Put the tasks in order, and then indicate the most difficult in terms of time, money, people, and other resources. Be as specific as possible, but recognize that at the outset, you will probably be able to list only the general tasks. For instance, a quality improvement group might have these tasks on its list: (1) define the problems, (2) collect data on the type and frequency of problems, (3) prioritize the problems and decide which one to work on, (4) collect data on the reasons for the problem (the method of data collection cannot be determined at this early stage since the problem has not been identified yet), (5) brainstorm possible changes to solve the problem, (6) establish objectives, (7) design and implement a trial to correct the problem, (8) establish ways to measure the objectives, (9) measure change, and (10) consider next steps.

Here is a case example about the early stage of group formation. The group's goal is to accomplish a complex project that requires people who have different expertise and come from a range of departments in the organization. Think about what you would do in this situation to create a high-performing group.

Example: New Electronic Records System

Many public school systems and universities have made the transition from paper guidance records to electronic records. Suppose that you work in a large, urban public school system that has been using a mainframe records database for the past thirty years with few updates. The system superintendent formed a task force to create a Web-based PC system. You are the director of the information technology department that programs the new software, customizing it for your system. You have a group of wonderful programmers working under you. To determine how you will proceed, reflect on these questions:

- What do you need to know about the school system?
- What do you need to know about student records?
- Who will use the system?
- Will the entire system be completed at once or in parts? Will you continue to develop it after the first version is implemented?
- Will the system have to interact with other databases in the school system or the city?
- How will you deal with guidance counselors and faculty who are not computer savvy or prefer the old system?
- Who needs to be on your implementation group? Why?
- What systems do other school districts use that you can learn from?

You want people who know the functions of the system and the technology, so you select the following small group: a guidance counselor and a faculty member, both of whom you know well and have worked with before; three programmers on your staff; an administrator who makes decisions about what other software is used in the institution; and a faculty trainer. You are the chair.

Now think about your group members. Do they all know each other? Have they worked together before? Do they get along and understand each other's daily functions and skills? What unique knowledge and perspectives do they bring to the table? Here's what you think about each of them.

The faculty member uses the computer for some online course work but prefers one-to-one small group and classroom communication. He was coerced into using the online teaching software by his supervisor. Recently he had a negative experience when his computer had a virus on it and a programmer on your staff unwittingly deleted one of his online lectures while trying to deal with the virus. The computer's hard drive was lost in the attempt, and the faculty member, who did not know any better, lost all of his online lectures, which he had saved only on his hard drive and had not loaded them to the online program. As it happens, this was one of the programmers you selected for the development group. The faculty member is astounded that he is now on a group to create a new student records system with the same IT staff member who lost his course preparations and cost him many hours of recomposing his work. You are a bit worried that the faculty member, like other faculty in the system, will not want to learn a new process and will not want to work with a person he feels may have substandard programming skills.

The administrator has worked at the school for years and has facilitated the IT department's growth. However, she is more familiar with the cost of the system than its use.

The guidance counselor is ready to toss the current system. It is slow, requires entering codes to get data (it is not user friendly), and takes considerable time to generate reports and print records. He is looking forward to a better system but has let you know that he has to do his current job and will not have much time for the group. Nevertheless, he knows how important the new system will be to his department.

The faculty trainer teaches faculty and counselors how to use DVD players, basic classroom computer programs, some teaching classroom techniques, and basic teaching skills, such as writing daily plans that meet the state competencies and time management of the administrative aspects of teaching. He is a little upset that he has been appointed to this group because he knows it will eat up his free time when he would rather be surfing the Web for new ways to use cooperative learning in the classroom.

One other member of the group is an educational consultant who works in the state department of education and knows all of the rules and regulations for creating transcripts and maintaining permanent student records. Her time is tight, and she probably will not be able to attend regular group meetings. In fact, you may need to schedule group meetings around her schedule. You wonder how others in the group will feel about this and wonder if she really needs to be a member of this group on a regular basis.

You have a lot of confidence in your IT group. You picked every member and know their strengths and weaknesses. You know how to design products to meet the needs of your clients as long as the clients provide a clear outline of what they want to do with the product and how it should function. You are easily angered by small-minded people who do not understand how complex programming can be, so you will have to guard your temper and sarcasm to be sure the group works cohesively.

It is 4:00 P.M. on a Tuesday afternoon. School is over for the day, and the building is emptying out. Your meeting is about to begin. What's your plan? Consider the following:

1. What do you know?

    a. Your goal is to develop a new electronic student records system.

    b. Your group consists of diverse people who have varied interests in this project.

    c. Scheduling meetings will be an issue if all members are to be present all the time (or even most).

    d. You meet at the end of the day. Everyone will be tired and maybe hungry.

2. What can you plan ahead of time?

    a. Write up the charge of the group so you can give everyone a copy—a concrete handout.

    b. Plan a way for members to get to know each other. They will learn about each other's abilities and interests, how they use student records, and what they know about data systems.

    c. Investigate what other institutions are doing about their student records. Find some examples of Web-based systems that you can describe to the group.

d. Communicate personally with each member before the meeting. They might say, "How long are we going to have to be here after hours? I have to get home," or, "I'm really sick of putting in extra time for someone else's convenience," or "This is great. I've been waiting for this to happen for years. I can't wait to get started."

e. In setting up a meeting schedule, respect the needs of your group members, and try to be flexible. Also, remind them that this is an important, costly project.

f. Collect some information about how the current grade reporting system works. Emphasize what works well and what does not.

3. What should you do at the first meeting and thereafter?

a. Hand out a copy of the charge of the committee.

b. Ask group members to introduce themselves and say why they feel they were chosen to be in this group. What skills do they bring to the group that will enable the group to do its work better? What is their understanding of the group's task?

c. Show some examples from other schools that have a system from the same software company. Consider whether any of these models would work here. What could the school adopt and what could it adapt? Should the group start from scratch? If the group chooses to adopt others' models, they will probably allow the school to use their computer code, saving time and money. But then the school may have to adapt its process to the software's capabilities.

d. Engage group members in discussion about the process. Ask someone to take notes and to distribute them to everyone soon after the meeting. Decide what the next steps will be.

e. In discussion, decide what kind of group work will take place. Will everyone work independently or together? Will the group split into smaller groups? Will more outside expertise be needed?

f. Make initial assignments (or let group members choose their assignments).

g. Be sure the group members know that you intend to follow up on assignments between meetings.

4. Plan to give feedback to each member to let them know if their performance is close to your and the group's expectations. You will offer public kudos when appropriate. If you have to give negative feedback, do it in private so that you do not hamper the receiver's motivation or willingness to work with the other group members.

At this early stage in what will be a complex process, you have concentrated on selecting group members to provide functional (end user) and technical knowledge. You have considered their vested interests and how well they are likely to get along. You have done some planning for the first meeting. You expect the group to structure the process. That is, you and the group members will determine what needs to get done and what the schedule will be. Their time and commitment may be a problem. The project may require lots more energy than they are willing to give.

This is how many project teams and task forces begin. Leaders try to find the right talent, with the expectation that if they have the right people, setting objectives, structuring the task, and establishing time lines will be easy. Group leaders need to pay attention to all three major components of a high-performing group: talent, time, and task. The leader's expectation in the school example was that the group would guide task and structure. Was this realistic? The following chapters will help you answer this question and structure your own group process by having a better understanding of leading, getting started, facilitating group performance, creating a learning group, and assessing process and outcome.

Summary

In this chapter, we outlined the three principal characteristics of a high-performing group: talent, time, and task. We examined the challenges of creating this group and how to determine the extent to which your group is high performing or has the potential to become high performing. We considered how to choose group members, recognizing the effects of member diversity on group process. We presented exercises to help you design a high-performing group. Keep the following points in mind:

- Be sure the group has talented members (those with the skills, knowledge, and background) to do the job. Group members need appropriate technical and interaction skills. Interaction skills such as the ability to collaborate, resolve conflicts, and negotiate are particularly hard to assess. Leaders rely on prior experience with members, recommendations from others they trust, and background information to select group members.

- Develop a shared vision—that is, a common understanding of the purpose for the group and why these members have been selected for it. Recognize whose responsibility it is if the group fails. Identify and discuss differences in perspective. Discuss the challenges the group is likely to confront. Determine how the group will operate—the rules it will follow.

- Discuss different ways of making a decision, and decide which one or ones the group will use for different types of decisions. For instance, the group may want to work toward consensus most of the time, use motions and voting when a consensus cannot be reached, and require a two-thirds majority vote for allocating money.

- Avoid groupthink by encouraging honest expressions of opinion and not overemphasizing the importance of consensus during the group process.

- Be sure that the group has clear objectives, a common understanding of how to achieve them, and ways to assess whether they have met their objectives. Be sure that the task itself is clear and significant (something the members understand and think of as worthwhile) and that work methods and assignments are clear and can be accomplished in the time allowed. Also, be sure there is a way to evaluate the quality of the group's product and that all the members and others, such as users of the group product, know how good it is.

- Be sure that the members have the time to spend on the task. If they are too busy doing other things or if other things are more important to them, chances are they will not be effective group members. Also, be sure that the group has sufficient time to work together—that meetings are at convenient times and that members schedule time to work on the group's task between meetings.

- Assess your group's potential to become high performing by assessing members' characteristics, the clarity of purpose and time frame (likelihood of meeting deadlines), the challenges and obstacles the group is likely to face, and the degree of collaboration and empowerment.

- Review the action steps we suggested above to structure the task and time for the group as it gets to work, for instance, helping the members get to know each other.

- Consider the value of group member diversity when you form the group. Group composition (for example, the percentage of men in the group) can be important in determining the extent to which each person adds value and influencing how the group will operate.

Chapter 3

PLANNING YOUR GROUP'S DEVELOPMENT

When you begin leading a group, you might wonder, What can I expect to happen in the group? Should I assume that my group members are as motivated as I am to work on this project or committee? What if my group members do not know each other well? Is this a problem?

In this chapter, we cover how small, short-term groups develop. We describe groups from individual, group, and organizational perspectives and how groups are dynamic systems. This provides a lens for understanding group development and gives examples of how different groups evolve—sometimes muddling through, other times following a steady progression. Sometimes groups get stuck and do not make much progress until they are close to the deadline. We suggest ways to help you overcome barriers and keep your group on track.

After reading this chapter, you will be able to:

- Distinguish between individual, group, and organizational characteristics that influence how your group operates.
- Define a group as a living system that has input, throughput, output, and feedback components that you can influence.
- Recognize the five stages of group development: forming, storming, norming, performing, and adjourning.
- Help your group learn and improve as it moves from one stage to the next.
- Accurately estimate the time your group needs to complete its work.

- Recognize when your group is floundering and when it is ready to focus on a specific direction, goal, and process.
- Compare your group's progress to your expectations.
- Use clear timetables, assignments, and frequent communication.
- Facilitate group process through collaborative behavior, joint decision making, and information exchange.

Understanding Groups from an Individual, Group, and Organizational Perspective

As a lens to understand group development, we begin by considering the group from the individual, group, and organizational perspectives and how a group operates as a dynamic system. In thinking about the type of group you are leading and its characteristics, you naturally focus on the task you need to get done, your time line, and how your members are going to work together. You can also think of the group from the perspective of each individual member: each individual's abilities, personality, and motivation that shape his or her behavior in the group. In addition, you can recognize the context in which your group is operating: the organization's expectations and demands, the resources and encouragement groups such as yours receive, and the consequences of your group's performance to the success or failure of the organization. All three levels (individual, group, and organization) can influence the outcomes of your group.

Understanding Groups from Individual, Group, and Organizational Perspectives

J. Richard Hackman (2003), an organizational psychologist at Harvard University, has studied orchestras, airplanes, and hospitals to demonstrate the importance of understanding how individual, social, and contextual factors influence what happens in a group. He has three examples from his research:

- *Orchestras:* Studying seventy-eight professional orchestras around the world, Hackman and his colleagues found that many of these groups, which traditionally had been all male, were beginning to hire more women. They found that player attitudes and the way the orchestras functioned deteriorated significantly as the proportion of women increased. An increase in the number of women seemed to generate tensions and problems for both the orchestras as groups and the individual players, and these difficulties worsened until the gender composition became relatively balanced (approaching 40 percent women). When the researchers explored further, they discovered that the difficulties were due mainly to the perceptions of men in these orchestras. The gender effects were based on the perceptions and experiences of the veteran men more than those of the entering women. One or two women in an orchestra were little threat to the homogeneous life of a mostly male orchestra, particularly if the women played instruments that were considered typical for women, such as harp or flute. However, women's presence in larger numbers encroaching on the high-status turf that had previously been a male bastion disrupted the social dynamics of the orchestra and often produced stressful conflicts. Context also mattered. The negative effects of women were worse in West German orchestras because the gender cultures in the orchestras, paralleling the representation of women in the national workforce, did not welcome women. In contrast, in the United States, equal employment opportunity regulations in the workforce and blind auditions for player selection (for example, listening to recordings), attitudes and operations, were more positive.

- *Airline cockpit crews:* A study of three hundred crews who flew nine different types of aircraft found that crew-level variables (the design of the flying task and the design of the crew itself), which should determine how members work together as a self-correcting performing unit, showed almost no differences across airlines' performance records. So the researchers looked deeper at the individuals and the context. Here, individual differences did not seem to matter. For instance, captains' leadership style measured by in-flight observations and self-report surveys did not vary much among airlines. However, the organizational context did matter. This included variables such as adequacy of material resources, clarity of performance objectives, recognition and reinforcement for excellent crew performance, availability of educational and technical assistance, and availability of informational resources. Together these variables accounted for substantial differences in the performance of the airlines. The most economically successful airlines were highest on measures of these characteristics, and the struggling domestic carrier was lowest. The context measures also were related to pilots' self-reported satisfaction with job security, compensation, and management, although there was no indication that pilot satisfaction affected their performance.

• *Hospital patient care teams*: Hackman's study, conducted in two hospitals of eight patient care teams of about forty members each, showed the unexpected finding that teams that were especially well structured and managed had significantly more medication errors than other units. Unlike the airline crews that were highly structured, the nurse managers of the patient care teams had considerable latitude in how they designed and managed their teams. It turned out that the nurse managers had the authority to tailor their units to fit their personal managerial preferences. Some preferred an informal, open climate, whereas others preferred a highly structured climate. In open climates, nurse managers actively encouraged discussion of errors and learning from them. In the structured, authoritarian climates, nurse managers signaled that errors should be suppressed.

Based on these research findings, consider the impact of individual differences, group structure (such as role assignments), and organizational context on your own group. For example, to what extent do organizational and environmental conditions determine or constrain what issues you have to deal with and the freedom your group has in what you do and how you do it? To what extent do the members' roles shape how they contribute to the group—for instance, when and how often they can express their opinions or make decisions on their own? To what extent do characteristics of individual members affect what they do and how they react to other group members, and does this influence the progress of the group?

The Group as a Living System

A system has five components: environment, input, throughput, output, and feedback. Individuals, group characteristics, and environment (context) determine input, which leads to process and outcomes, as depicted in Figure 3.1. Feedback may affect the environment, as well as future inputs and process. Living systems are dynamic in that they are continuously evolving. You can consider an individual, group, or organization to be a *system*.

Holly Arrow of the University of Oregon and colleagues Joseph McGrath at the University of Illinois and Jennifer Berdahl at the University of California at Berkeley conceptualized groups as open,

Figure 3.1 A Systems Model of Group Process

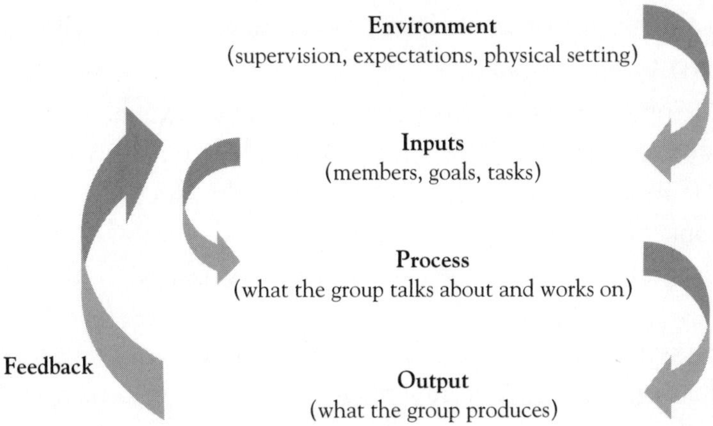

Environment
(supervision, expectations, physical setting)

Inputs
(members, goals, tasks)

Process
(what the group talks about and works on)

Feedback

Output
(what the group produces)

complex systems that interact with their environment, are influenced by the individual characteristics of their members, change
over time, and use information (feedback) to adjust to varied pressures
(Arrow, McGrath, & Berdahl, 2000). Specifically, they described
groups as follows:

- Groups are open and complex systems that interact with
  smaller systems (group members) embedded within them
  and the larger system (organizations) of which they are a part.
  Group boundaries are fuzzy, meaning that the boundaries distinguish them from other individuals and groups but allow
  interaction and mutual influence.

- Groups are social systems within physical, time-bound, social,
  cultural, and organizational environments.

- Groups acquire members, projects, and resources from their
  environments. They reach outside the group to access a rich
  array of resources. Being willing, able, and encouraged to
  reach outside the group boundaries to draw on these resources
  can enrich the group process.

- Groups negotiate exchanges of their members who belong
  to multiple groups simultaneously. They use their members'
  knowledge and skills and pay them salaries and other benefits.

- Groups are complex systems that are neither rigidly ordered
  nor highly disordered. They tend to increase in complexity
  over time.

- Groups have the capacity for self-correction. Members have
  an idea of the preferred state or path. They pay attention to
  information (feedback) indicating that the group as a whole or
  some of its members are drifting off course (because of internal
  dynamics or outside forces) and need to get back on track.

So as a leader, recognize that your group is dynamic, will change,
is influenced by the environment, and should not be constrained by

rigid boundaries but rather should be permeable and benefit from exchange with other groups.

Stages of Group Development

In the first two chapters, we gave you some ideas about understanding your group, in particular, its purpose, characteristics, degree of challenge and uncertainty, how it will operate, and the extent to which members will cooperate with each other as they work together toward common goals. Here, we focus on how group processes unfold over time.

There are a variety of models of group development (Smith, 2001). Some focus on the cyclical, pendulum-like nature of group process as members seem to make progress and then revert back, revisiting discussions and decisions they already had. Other models hold that groups make little real progress until a deadline approaches (Gersick, 1989). Still other models are linear, suggesting that groups move from one stage to the next in a logical, continual progression. Each model is likely to have some applicability in helping us understand how groups work. We consider stages that many groups go through, sometimes in a continual progression, other times moving back and forth between stages. Understanding these stages will help you as the leader move the group through each stage and manage the transition between stages.

Most groups follow a five-stage process: forming, storming, norming, performing, and adjourning (Tuckman, 1965; Tuckman & Jensen, 1977). Of course, groups vary in how quickly they progress through each stage. All stages may happen during a course of one meeting, or each stage may take several meetings to unfold. Most groups progress quickly through the early stages. Some backtrack if they are not making progress and need to regroup. Think of these five stages as the life cycle of a group, but remember that the stages vary in length and depth, do not always occur in that order, and may reappear as new issues emerge.

Stage 1: Forming

This first stage, *forming*, sometimes called *inclusion*, is the time when the group comes together. Members meet each other for the first time as a group. They meet the leader, or they may elect a leader from the membership. (The group could remain leaderless until one leader, or possibly more than one, emerges over time based on who exerts the most energy and shapes the direction of the group.) During this opening stage, members are likely to feel anxious and uncertain. They will be polite to each other and careful about what they say. As leader, you take center stage. Members expect you to facilitate introductions, describe what the group can and should accomplish, and set expectations for later meetings.

If you are responsible for recruiting members, your challenge is to find people who have the needed skills and knowledge, the time available to work with the group, the motivation to stick with the task, and a personality that is compatible with those of the other members.

In general, your challenge during this first stage is to make people feel comfortable and provide some information about why the group was formed. Come to the first meeting prepared to shape members' expectations and build their spirits. You can be expressive about why this is going to be a great group and all the wonderful things the group members will work on together. Make the members feel comfortable by setting a realistic schedule and describing realistic goals. Also, explain how you would like the group to operate, for instance, that you want members to participate actively, express their ideas and opinions, make decisions, and shape the group's goals and work activities. This assumes that the group members are indeed able, and want, to participate at that level and that they have meaningful contributions to make. If not, the members may want a leader who is going to make this easy for them by structuring the work, giving them assignments, setting due dates, and then collecting and integrating everyone's work.

Stage 2: Storming

During *storming,* members express their feelings about what they expect the group to do and how they want it to operate. It is the time when the tension between members' vested interests and the group goal becomes evident. The stage may be brief if you, as the leader, have recognized members' capabilities, motivation, interests, and expectations from the start, and the members know and respect each other. However, if you misread group members' expectations or motivation or did not give them enough credit for their abilities and experience, this is likely to be a difficult and possibly long stage. Members who have not yet gotten to know you or the other members well may express their frustration with you as leader, clarify their own goals, and assert independence from you. They may get together among themselves in coalitions before the meeting so that they have a unified show of force—letting you know in no uncertain terms that others feel the same way and have similar interests that are not in line with your goals or work methods.

Your challenge in the storming stage is to be open to what the group has to say. You can ask the group members for their ideas about the mission and goals for the group. They can discuss the vision for the final product rather than being told what it is. You can facilitate the emergence of a shared vision for the group that members can commit to and feel is worth their time and energy.

Stage 3: Norming

This is the time when members gain trust in you as the leader and in each other. They discuss and agree on ways to structure the work and communicate with each other. Although this might change over time, the initial feeling that they agree on goals and how to accomplish them will give them a sense of routine and comfort. Conflicts that arose during the storming phase are resolved and a sense of cohesiveness emerges—that they are all in this together, respect each other, and are looking forward to working together. Members have confidence that they are accepted by other group members. They are willing to say how they really feel, and when they disagree, they say so and are open to negotiations.

Of course, sometimes the group has not totally concluded the storming stage, and the members may raise unpleasant disagreements and unresolved conflicts. In this case, you need to recognize the need for backtracking.

The group may return to this norming stage from time to time, with, you hope, little storming as a prelude. This is the time to review how well the group is working and discuss changes in goals, deadlines, and work methods that will get the group back on track.

Your challenge during norming is to acquire the resources the group needs to achieve its goals. There is no point in setting a goal that cannot be met because the money, facilities, or other resources are not available. You can give members confidence that they are on the right track, that others agree with what they are doing, and that they should be able to meet their objectives. You can reinforce their confidence by setting a timetable for goals and a meeting schedule that recognizes most, if not all, the members' availability.

Stage 4: Performing

This is the stage when the work gets done: the group members are engaged in the task and working in earnest to achieve the group's goals. Here, your challenge is to continue to provide the resources you promised. You may be most helpful by facilitating transactions, for instance, planning group meetings, setting agendas, taking and distributing minutes (or being sure that one of the members does this, for instance, the elected or appointed secretary), and facilitating group discussions. Be sure that everyone is involved and that one or two people do not monopolize the conversation. Monitor the group's progress, and let members know how close they are to important milestones. Also, help group members think about what they are doing and whether it is working. Help the group adjust to any changes in membership, with some people dropping out and new members joining the group at different stages. If the group is getting bogged down and not meeting its objectives, help reformulate goals, assignments, and work methods (a return to norming).

Stage 5: Adjourning

The last stage is finishing the work of the group, for instance, holding the event the group planned, presenting the design for a new product the group developed, or sending in the funds the group raised.

You can hold a postmortem with the group to ask the members to reflect on how they did. This is when you can give members feedback about their performance as individuals and give the group feedback. You can facilitate a discussion about group performance, asking the members to express how they felt about the group, what the group learned about how to accomplish the task at hand, and what the members learned about working together.

Now consider what is happening in each stage: what the members do and what you do as the group leader (Table 3.1).

Let's see how these stages unfold. We will take two examples: a chamber of commerce and a corporate training committee.

Table 3.1 Stages of Group Development

Stages of Group Development	What's Happening: Members . . .	What the Leader Can Do: Leader can . . .
Stage 1: Forming	• Meet each other, some for the first time. • Meet the leader; may elect the leader. • Feel anxious and uncertain. • Act polite to each other. • Expect the leader to facilitate introductions, describe what the group can do, and set the stage for later meetings.	• Find people who have the needed skills and knowledge, the time available to work with the group, the motivation, and compatibility. • Make members feel comfortable and provide some information about the group.

(Continued)

Table 3.1 Stages of Group Development, Continued

Stages of Group Development	What's Happening: Members . . .	What the Leader Can Do: Leader can . . .
		• Come to the meeting prepared to shape members' expectations and build their spirits. • Describe why this is going to be a great group and all the wonderful things the group members will accomplish. • Set a realistic schedule and describe realistic goals. • Explain how the group can operate.
Stage 2: Storming	• Express their feelings about how they want the group to operate. • Express their frustration with the leader. • Clarify their own goals. • Assert independence from leader. • Get together among themselves in coalitions before the meeting so that they have a unified show of force. • Let the leader know that others feel the same way and have similar interests that are not in line with the leader's goals or work methods.	• Remain open to group input. • Ask the group members for their ideas about the mission and goals for the group. • Discuss the vision for the final product. • Facilitate the emergence of a shared vision that members can commit to and feel is worth their time and energy. • Make sure the group stays on track and doesn't stray too far from the original goals that brought the group together in the first place. • Exercise good negotiation skills (see Appendix B).

Stages of Group Development	What's Happening: Members . . .	What the Leader Can Do: Leader can . . .
Stage 3: Norming	• Gain trust in the leader and each other. • Discuss and agree on ways to structure the work and communicate with each other. • Agree on goals and how to accomplish them. • Gain a sense of routine and comfort. • Resolve conflicts that arose during the storming stage. • Develop a sense of cohesiveness (a feeling that "we are all in this together"). • Have confidence that they are accepted by other group members. • Are willing to say how they really feel. • Express disagreements. • Are open to negotiations about goals and methods.	• Acquire the resources the group needs to achieve their goals. • Give members confidence that they are on the right track, that others agree with what they are doing, and that they should be able to meet their objectives. • Set a timetable for goals and a meeting schedule that recognizes most, if not all, members' availability.
Stage 4: Performing	• Get work done. • Exert energy. • Achieve group goals.	• Provide the promised resources. • Facilitate transactions, for instance, planning group meetings, setting agendas, taking and distributing minutes, and facilitating group discussions. • Be sure that everyone is involved and that one or two members do not monopolize the

(Continued)

Table 3.1 Stages of Group Development, Continued

Stages of Group Development	What's Happening: Members . . .	What the Leader Can Do: Leader can . . .
		discussions (for example, go around the room and ask each person to speak; give each person a time limit, for instance, two minutes).
		• Deal with difficult people, for example, those who do not give others a chance to speak (you might say, "Let's hear from someone else," and then call on another group member).
		• Monitor the group's progress, and let members know how close they are to important milestones.
		• Help group members reflect on what they are doing and whether it is working.
		• Help the group adjust to any changes in membership.
		• Initiate a transformation when the group gets bogged down; return to the norming stage, reformulate goals, assignments, and work methods.
Stage 5: Adjourning	• Finish the work of the group, whatever it happens to be. • Process what worked and did not.	• Hold a postmortem with the group to assess what went right and what went wrong.

Stages of Group Development	What's Happening: Members . . .	What the Leader Can Do: Leader can . . .
	• Offer suggestions for solving problems differently (focus on the problem or issue, not the individual).	• Give members feedback about their performance as individuals. • Give the group feedback. • Ask members to express how they felt about the group. • Help the members recognize what they learned as individuals and what the group learned about how to work together, what the group learned about how to accomplish the task at hand, and what the members learned about working together.

Example: Rejuvenating the Chamber of Commerce

Ron Williams, a business owner, was just elected president of the chamber of commerce, and his goal was to rejuvenate the chamber and do more to promote local business. The challenge for him was that several seasoned officers had moved or closed their businesses and were no longer part of the group; therefore, he needed to work with inexperienced officers of the chamber to build a cohesive group and develop programs to support business growth.

The forming stage went pretty quickly. Introductions went smoothly. Members of the group introduced themselves and described their backgrounds. This quickly led to the storming stage, with members expressing very different perspectives of what needed to be done. The vice president for programs, Sheila Jenkins, thought that what worked in the past should be continued in the future and that basically nothing new was needed. Several others felt strongly that new approaches had to be taken to recruit new members and be more active in community service to show that businesses were giving back to the community. These seemingly endless discussions went on meeting after meeting for several months. (The executive board met twice a month, and the full chamber met once a month at a luncheon.) Storming seemed to become the norm for this group. However, the fast-approaching deadline jogged the group into the performing stage. As the holidays approached, the president suggested that the chamber not only fund the decorations on Main Street, as was usual, but that they also plan a "Christmas Carol in the Streets" program with the local community theater and combine this with a holiday sale campaign. This idea hit a responsive chord in the group. Members felt that this would draw business away from the malls. The group worked quickly to make plans, set goals and timetables, and find donations of the needed resources. After months of discussion, performing was underway in just a single meeting. Time pressure helped get people to commit to a target and plan of action. Subcommittees were established to bring off this one event that was ultimately successful. It was not without some unexpected problems, of course. For instance, one member did not come through with some promised contributions of signs and food.

The question then became what to do next. Ron's task was to build on the successful experience and strengthen working relationships and avoid another round of endless discussions and disagreements. This could be the foundation for more ambitious programs to increase business in the town.

Example: Determining Staff Training Needs for the Corporate Training Committee

The leader of a corporate training committee in a manufacturing plant was a midlevel supervisor in engineering and design. The director of human resources at the plant asked if the supervisor would chair a committee to determine staff training needs. Part of the goal was to help managers and all employees recognize and value the importance of ongoing training to keep up with their field and be sure the plant was as efficient as possible.

This group had a very different experience compared to the chamber of commerce. The corporate training committee consisted of two union representatives, a computer technology expert, a training department manager, a clerical employee, and a plant supervisor, Hank Johnson, who chaired the group. The purpose was to determine training needs for clerical, technical, and shop floor employees. The group seemed to get off to an excellent start—the forming stage. The group members, who previously did not know each other well except as casual acquaintances, seemed congenial and happy to be participating in the committee. During the first meeting, the training manager, April Greenstein, suggested that everyone needed basic computer skills in today's world. The computer expert jumped right in to explain why this was important and to suggest that they sponsor a general training program to give everyone basic knowledge of how to use a computer for word processing, spreadsheets, and the Internet. Everyone agreed instantly. This seemed too good to be true. Hank asked several people to volunteer for a subcommittee to outline what the course would be and report to the group at the next meeting. The group seemed to have skipped the storming stage and were moving into norming and performing.

At that next meeting, the subcommittee presented a realistic, generic outline. Then one of the union representatives, Sheila, asked how this would benefit people on the shop floor. She wondered out loud whether this was an attempt to prepare people for a layoff. Would they need to find work elsewhere? How would these general computer skills be useful in the different manufacturing jobs? Computer-controlled robots were being used in different parts of the manufacturing process, but they were highly specialized procedures. A one-size-fits-all training program would not be useful if the goal was really to improve operations. This discussion led to a major argument about directions the group should take, what training was really needed, and who was calling the shots. The group had reverted to storming, which is not unusual, especially as a group is still trying to work out what it will do. The union people kept coming back to the question about whether this was really a setup by management. Members of the group did not say so directly, but some people felt that the group leader could not be trusted. April, the training manager, suggested that the group take a step back. Maybe the committee should conduct a needs analysis instead of assuming that the answer was that everyone needed computer skills.

The group leader asked everyone to calm down and went around the room to ask each person in turn to express an opinion about the direction for the committee. Everyone had a chance to speak. To a member, they all thought that they did not know what type of training could benefit the company and the employees, and they did not know how to find out. The training expert explained that there were several ways they could do this, starting by interviewing people in different jobs throughout the plant. A subcommittee was established to write some interview questions. With a process for performing, the group now seemed focused.

The next meetings concentrated on developing the interview questions, assigning committee members to conduct the interviews, and reviewing results. The interviews showed that several groups in the plant could benefit from technical and interpersonal training. A program of courses would be developed, some to take place in the plant classroom during company time and some to be available online that employees could take on their own time at home or in the plant's small computer room. During the course of a year of biweekly meetings, the committee established a process for developing new courses, monitoring their implementation by the training department, assessing their value by tracking who participated and how they applied what they learned on the jobs and in their lives outside of work, and collecting needs data periodically to suggest new courses.

Instead of adjourning, the committee became an ongoing advisory committee for the human resource and training department. Overall, the corporate training committee learned how to collect information that would inform their efforts. The first time around suggested a direction and taught the members about how to collect ongoing data to assess learning outcomes in the plant and guide future training.

Both of these committees were eventually successful, but not without initial conflict and frustration. The leaders in both groups faced the challenge of listening to diverse points of view, airing opinions and disagreements, and then generating consensus around a course of action. Members in both groups learned about how to work with each other effectively, although this was a somewhat painful experience initially.

These are two reasonably positive examples. The committee process does not always go so well. Members may lose interest and not show up for meetings. One or two members may collude to usurp the leader's authority and take the group in an entirely different direction from its original purpose. An argumentative, arrogant member can alienate other members and cause chaos. These problems require different leadership strategies, and there are ways to avoid them altogether. We address how leaders face such problems in Chapters Four and Seven.

Differences in Groups in How the Stages Unfold

Groups differ in their patterns of development. Not all follow a steady progression. Forming, storming, and norming may happen very quickly, perhaps during the course of the initial meeting, or the group might skip storming altogether, at least at first. After the group gets to work, disagreements may evoke a storming pattern that the group needs to resolve before it can be productive. Alternatively, the group might not emerge from norming, floundering without clear purpose or direction until time to get work done becomes tight.

For example, a group might establish a consistent pattern of operating. Members may have gotten to know each other, and they begin to hold weekly meetings and address routine business or hold general discussions about whatever they are supposed to be planning, organizing, or producing. They do not make much progress but also feel no pressure to do so. A sudden and radical change or event might jolt them out of their complacent pattern. This is likely to happen at the group's midpoint, when members realize the group has not made progress and something must be done. Awareness of time deadlines can focus the group's attention and stun them into new ways of acting.

Another example might be when the initial structure of the group forms quickly, for instance, members agree on who the leader is and the leader's role. Further structure emerges as group members volunteer for or are assigned to different roles. However, over time, members may contest and renegotiate the structure and their assignments.

The pace of these stages varies from one group to another. Some groups move quickly through the stages, and others take longer. Groups actively create and adjust their structure and interrelationships among members.

Learning During the Transition Stages

Periods of change and instability are periods of learning. As groups move from storming through norming to performing, and sometimes back again, they develop new ways of operating, handling difficult situations, and overcoming barriers. These stage transitions, often brought about by some event (a disagreement, a new idea, a new goal or demand, or something else that is unexpected), are a time for forming patterns of interrelationships within the group that are maintained after the event has passed. They become part of the group's collective memory. The members learn something about each other and how they interact. They learn what worked and what did not, and because they share the experience, these patterns of interaction solidify, at least until they are no longer effective or needed.

Estimating the Time Frame

A common problem in groups is that they underestimate the time required to complete a task or achieve a goal. The less time there is available, the more focused they are and the more likely they are to estimate the time required accurately. And the more time they have available, the more likely they are to underestimate what is required: "We have plenty of time. This is a piece of cake. Not to worry." These tend to be famous last words. If you fall behind, you might wonder how you can extend the deadline for the group. Of course, if you start with the idea that the deadline can always be extended, this might be the kiss of death. In other words, starting the group with the understanding that it is okay to fail is a bad way to begin. If clear objectives are established with each member understanding his or her role, reaching the group's goal should be possible. If the group discovers information that indicates the goal is unrealistic, the information should be presented to the person who gave the original directive—well ahead of the deadline, if possible. For example, the group can approach the supervisor and explain the difficulties that the group members are facing to see if additional resources can be provided so that they can reach their goal by the deadline. The supervisor might have ideas about how to proceed, including replacing the leader or group members.

Midway Transition

Generally deadlines create a driving force. The leader and group members must recognize the need for a transition about midway through the timetable for the project.

The Midpoint Transition

Connie Gersick (1989), a researcher at the University of California at Los Angeles, studied how groups pace themselves when they have a time limit to complete a creative task. Studying eight groups, each with three or four M.B.A. students engaged in a simulated organizational project to construct a product for a client, she discovered that there is a midpoint or transition point in a group's work. Before the mid-point, group members brainstorm and gather information. The process is more analytical. Members might go outside the group to get the information or flounder in discussions within the group. However, around the midpoint, when group members realize that time is fleeting and the deadline is near, the process becomes more creative. The group tends to bring closure to information gathering and discussion and are inspired to move ahead. The pace and qual-ity of the work change as decisions are made about a concrete plan of action, which is then enacted.

Groups sometimes fail at their objectives. Gersick found that if a group continues the pre-midpoint process of open discussion after the midpoint, the floundering does not stop. A concrete plan does not emerge until too late, and the task is not completed on time. This may happen because the members do not recognize the time limitation, or they may have a weak or unpopular leader who is unable to help the group make the transition at the midpoint.

As group leader, you might want to plan a transition midway into the group process so you are able to meet their deadlines. This might be a break followed by a "where are we now" progress discussion fol-lowed by "what should we do now." The idea is to refocus the group members' attention away from free-flowing discussion and expression of ideas to concrete goals and actions that are needed now.

Supporting the Group's Process

In Chapter One, we distinguished group purpose, product, and process. Process is the heart of what the group does. It consists of three elements: (1) getting started and making transitions—members working on planning, analysis, and goal setting types of activities; (2) doing things—members focusing on goal accomplishment, coordinating their activities, and monitoring group progress; and

(3) working on relationships—members managing their conflicts, motivation, and feelings about the group and about each other (Marks, Mathieu, & Zaccaro, 2001).

Using these three elements, how good is your group process? Rate your group's process using a five-point scale where 1 = low agreement and 5 = high agreement:

Getting Started and Handling Transitions

Members of my group discuss . . .

_____ Our vision for our group's performance (what we want the group to accomplish)

_____ Others' expectations for our group

_____ Our plans for accomplishing our vision

_____ What we can do day-to-day to make our performance vision a reality

Activities

Members of my group . . .

_____ Take the time we need to share information

_____ Actively learn from one another

_____ Effectively communicate with each other

Relationships

Members of my group . . .

_____ Create an environment of openness and trust

_____ Treat each other with respect

_____ Think in terms of what is best for the group

If the results of this "thought" survey are positive, you are probably on the right track. If not, the results may help you pinpoint how you can change your group's process to make more progress.

Are your plans clear? Do you have actions underway? Are relationships hindering the group's efforts (personality clashes, disagreements, arguments), and would it help to ask the group to talk about how well they are working together?

Complete this survey periodically. Your group will have different needs at different times, so the process evolves as members get to know each other and work together.

Group Process as a Cycle

What a group does affects what the group learns, and group outcomes affect later group goals. This can be viewed as a cycle of goals, process, outcomes, and learning that repeats over time.

The leader's and group's vision of outcomes and how to achieve them shapes the process that emerges. Consider how this works in music. Musicians may first read a score without playing it, listen to a recording, and then sight-read it. They consider its high points, its climaxes, themes, modulations, and the kind of group that will be performing the music. The musicians "hear" it all at the beginning. Even after playing it through just once, seasoned musicians have an idea of how the piece goes. They reflect on the sounds and consider a retrospective interpretation of how the music will go once it has been practiced and readied for the audience. They form ideas of how to practice sections, particularly difficult spots. This reflective, interpretive process becomes an internal performance goal toward which the musicians aim as individual performers or as an ensemble.

In musical groups, the conductor develops an image for the piece and may convey this image to the ensemble as they begin rehearsal, or maybe not. The conductor may direct the process from his or her internalized conceptualization and let things unfold and evolve, perhaps in a different direction from his or her initial conceptualization. On the one hand, communicating the vision beforehand may build trust and a shared vision among the ensemble members, who ultimately depend on each other to perform in harmony. On the other hand, not communicating the vision may provide flexibility and flu-idity to the process as long as the conductor is willing to bend his or her initial vision of the outcome and process.

Similarly, in groups charged with any task, the leader and members must form a vision of the end as the group begins. Of course, their visions may not agree, and some members' visions may not be as clear as others. Group members conceptualize their goals and divvy up the workload so as to practice their way toward the ending. Research, writing, and creating—all sorts of interactive communication—move the group closer toward its mission. The leader needs to outline clear directives to the group or help the group members form objectives for the group. These objectives are metaphorically like musicians' first glances of what the end result will be. Unclear objectives can cause a group to flounder. The result may be mediocre, meeting no one's expectations.

To continue our analogy to music performance, musicians sometimes ask, "How do I know if I'm playing a piece correctly?" How does a musician define a "correct" interpretation? In many ways, it is more difficult for a soloist to develop the sense of an acceptable interpretation. Until musicians have a certain level of expertise, they may have trouble hearing themselves objectively enough to recognize a distortion and correct it. Listening to a taped performance of oneself playing may help. Playing for another person who has more expertise or even a peer with a fresh point of view provides the opportunity for feedback and the corrections of distortions. Even expert performers take care to abide by the "rules"—the musical score—in an effort to avoid distortions.

Group leaders can be like solo performers. They can take the opportunity to bounce ideas around with their peers, or they can go it alone—like the musician with the tape recorder—until they have confidence that their goals are within the acceptable limitations of their environment. The leader's challenge, though, is not acting alone but rather getting members involved in this process.

As group process unfolds, members get to know each other better. Musicians who play in tight ensembles must understand their partners. Working in synchrony depends on knowing how your partners move, think, prepare, and practice and what they are likely to do under stress and pressure. What if your partners rush when they get nervous in a concert? If you are at the piano next to them and have not learned your part just a bit faster than you would ordinarily play it, they might get ahead of you in the music, causing the synchrony to break down.

Expectations and anticipation can help a group member work at the correct pace and prepare appropriate materials in an understandable and acceptable format for other group members to mold and shape. You cannot anticipate your fellow members unless you know them and what they are likely to do. The longer that group members work together, the better they are likely to anticipate each other's moves, making synchronous performance more likely.

Ensemble music provides built-in feedback to the musicians. Ensemble members, like members of any other group, offer fresh points of view and solutions to process. Honest, clear communication among members helps them clarify ideas and make decisions about what the next move should be. Some level of consensus between members is important for the work to move ahead. If a group member does not agree with the group, the same issue may need to be revisited each time the group meets. It is impossible to make real progress unless members are genuine in their consensus, trust, and acceptance. Still, as we found in Chapter Two, too much emphasis on consensus during group process can create groupthink, leading to faulty decisions. Thorough airing of ideas is important as the group progresses, but once it is time to make a final decision, consensus is important.

To summarize, as a leader, you need a clear vision of the group process: what members are doing and how well they are working together. As group members work with each other, they learn about their own and others' talents, attitudes, and personalities. They develop expectations about each other and the group, and they learn to anticipate their behaviors and actions. Honesty of purpose and direction, as well as openness in communications, are extremely important to protect the group's integrity and cohesiveness. Your task is to shape members' behaviors and expectations in ways that promote the group's purpose and product. Be a role model for clear and honest communication and giving and requesting feedback. Also, acknowledge when members agree, and address disagreements openly.

Assessing Group Progress

How will you know if your group is meeting its objectives? You need to work with the group members to establish ultimate objectives and hurdles that you want to achieve along the way. Tracking and assessing progress requires clear timetables, assignments, frequent communication, and clear benchmarks (measures of excellence).

Here is an example. After a natural disaster, a group of workers decides to help the victims and form a helping team. They have a deadline, since they are leaving for a conference in eight days, but they want to do something meaningful (send food and clothing, for example). None of the members has time to do this task alone, so they divvy up the responsibilities. One member owns a van and volunteers to drive whatever is collected to a central site, where it can be packed. He calls a delivery service and asks for an appointment for pickup. Another member agrees to make signs and post them, asking for clothing and packaged food drop-offs. Another member says she will send out a mass e-mail and help to collect items from the drop-off boxes. Two other members will get a cart and carry the items to the van. All members will meet at the packing site and help pack the items into boxes. The delivery service will help them meet their deadline. The group determined their deadline, defined the tasks that had to be done, and decided who would do what. Then they coordinated their actions with clear communications to be sure they met their objectives.

Let's say things went wrong. Five days into the project, no items had been dropped off in the collection boxes. How would the group have been able to determine and diagnose what the problem was? They would have had to review their initial plan—in particular, who was supposed to notify people to drop off items. Then they could see if that group member had carried out this obligation to the group. Group minutes would help keep track of tasks and responsibilities, even in this informal, self-organizing group. Maybe one group member became ill immediately after the meeting and was not able to send out e-mails or make flyers. As a result, no one knew about their project, and so no one dropped off the items. The diagnosis would indicate that the group member failed to communicate to the group, and due to this lack of communication, the group might have failed in achieving its objective. Once this is recognized, the group can decide with the errant member whether they can still carry out the original plan or whether it is too late to meet the deadline.

Notice that the group decides together with the ill group member how to proceed. The group could have decided to tell the group member he is no longer wanted in the group because of his failure to communicate, and some groups do this. This group acknowledged that a member made an error in failing to communicate but that the other group members also failed: they did not monitor the boxes frequently enough to notice the problem, and they did not notice that a group member was missing. Their diagnostic skills were poor. The members should have determined how they would monitor whether their responsibilities were carried out.

As your group develops, you must assess its progress. You will need measures and benchmarks such as dates by which you want to accomplish different tasks and levels of performance outcomes that you want to reach. This will allow you to compare what you have done to the group's objectives. If objectives are not being met (especially if none are being met), the group should talk about why this is happening and identify any obstacles that are preventing the group from meeting the group's objectives.

Building Group Cohesiveness

Cohesive groups are those in which the members are committed to the task, have pride in belonging to the group, and like one another, perhaps because they have worked with each other in the past, they know each other well, and feel comfortable with each other.

Think about the members of your group. Do they like belonging to the group? Do they like the activities they are working on? Have a discussion about this in the group. Ask about task cohesion: how well they like working together on the group's task. Then ask about interpersonal cohesion: how well they like each other. For instance, were they friends before they were members of the group? Have they become friends since joining the group? Do they generally get along with each other? Admittedly these are difficult issues to discuss. Nevertheless, asking these questions may help members focus on their common goals and recognize that their differences are really not important, or that they are after all, in which case group facilitation will be needed (a topic we cover in Chapter Six).

There are three elements to a cohesive group: (1) the level of collaborative behavior, (2) the quantity and quality of information exchanged, and (3) emphasis on joint decision making. Use the following scales to think about the components of group cohesion (from Simsek, Veiga, Lubatkin, & Dino, 2005):

Collaborative Behavior

On a scale from 1 (Strongly Disagree) to 5 (Strongly Agree), rate your group on the following items:

_____ When a group member is busy, other group members often volunteer to help manage the workload.

_____ Members are flexible about switching responsibilities to make things easier for each other.

_____ Members are willing to help each other complete jobs and meet deadlines.

Information Exchange

On a scale from 1 (Low Effectiveness) to 5 (High Effectiveness), rate your group on the following:

_____ Members share ideas.

_____ Members express their opinions openly.

_____ Members encourage each other's creativity and innovation.

_____ Members give and ask for feedback about their ideas.

Joint Decision Making

Use the same scale as you used for assessing collaborative behavior.

_____ Members usually let each other know when their actions affect another group member's work.

_____ Members have a clear understanding of the joint problems and needs of other group members.

_____ Members usually discuss their expectations of each other.

Consider using these scales at a group meeting. Have members complete the scales and discuss the results. From this discussion, talk about how the group members can improve their communication and work together more collaboratively.

Collaboration can be viewed more broadly than members helping each other. Edward Mone, vice president of organization development at Computer Associates, developed a workshop on group development in which he defines collaboration in terms of six dimensions: communication, openness, supportiveness, integrity, knowledge, and assistance (personal communication, October 26,

2006). All are necessary for meaningful collaboration. Group members need to be able to express ideas clearly, ask each other questions, and confirm when ideas are understood. They need to be willing to deal with problems openly and reserve judgment until all ideas surface. They need to place the group's goals above their individual agendas and encourage and defend each other. They need to be honest and trustworthy. They need to acquire and share new knowledge that will help the group. And they need to be proactive in offering to help fellow group members.

Facilitating Group Development

As we conclude this chapter, here are some ways you can help your group develop quickly. These methods are intended to stimulate member involvement, promote clear and honest communication, monitor progress, and generally sustain a group process that keeps the group focused on its goals. We say more in Chapter Five about ways to start a group and in Chapters Six and Seven how to improve group performance.

1. At the end of your first meeting, list your expectations. Have each group member do the same, and pass them to you. Read them privately. Summarize the differences and similarities at the next group meeting. List the differences, and rate their importance. Talk about the three most important differences.

2. Outline goals. Ask group members to list goals and project time lines for achieving them. Ask them to rate the extent of effort needed to accomplish each goal and indicate the probability that each can be accomplished. Discuss how the goals or time line (or both) need to be adjusted to make them more realistic. Revise each, and repeat the exercise. Depending on the size of your group, members might do this first individually (in a small group of two to four members), or in subgroups of two or three (in a larger group) and then report back to the whole group for discussion.

3. Ask each group member to list the things that need to be done to accomplish the task and to indicate how much time and effort each will take. Do a synthesis, and report back to the group next time. When the group meets again, discuss problem areas and make adjustments. Some groups will not have the time to do this. This exercise might be just a short part of the first meeting.

4. Consider whether the group has the resources, knowledge, and skills to be successful. If not, what can be done to get them?

5. After the group gets started, reevaluate whether it has the resources it needs to be successful. Do the group members have the expertise and knowledge they need? Do they know how to work together? Perhaps some training on communication and interpersonal relationships might help. (We say more about group learning and training in Chapter Seven.)

6. Ask group members to describe other similar efforts of which they had been a part. For those that worked well according to the group member, ask why, and list the points that contributed to positive functioning (for example, the meeting schedule was planned in advance so members knew when all the meetings would be held, minutes of each group meeting were kept and distributed to members before the next meeting, and votes were taken to make important decisions). For groups that did not go well, list the points that contributed to dysfunction (perhaps meetings went on too long, people could not agree on anything, some people went off on tangents or did not give others a chance to speak, the group did not stick to an agenda, or people made commitments they could not or did not keep). What can be done to ensure this group has the positive points and avoids the negative points? This might work best in groups that are going to meet periodically (say, biweekly or once a month) during an extended period of time, because they have ample time to reflect on their meetings.

However, all groups should take the time to think about group process. (We return to this topic in Chapter Eight in a discussion of assessing group process and outcomes.)

7. Determine the methods and measures the group needs to track its accomplishments.

8. Identify factors that will facilitate keeping the group on track—for example, frequent communication, clear minutes of group meetings that include records of who is supposed to do what by when, and time to review progress and make adjustments in goals and work methods.

9. Think about the number of meetings you are having. People do not want to waste their time, and the number of meetings and the length of the meetings affect group members' satisfaction and feelings of well-being.

Meetings Affect People's Attitudes About Their Jobs

People do not want to waste their time in meetings. But given that so much work gets done in meetings, this is likely to be a major portion of an individual's workday. Indeed, time spent in meetings, the number of meetings one attends, and the perceived effectiveness of these meetings are related to job satisfaction and feelings of well-being. An online survey of 676 full-time employees in a variety of employment sectors (finance, health care, manufacturing, retail, and public administration) in the United States and the United Kingdom asked about their experiences attending prescheduled meetings during a typical week (Rogelberg, Leach, Warr, & Burnfield, 2006). Respondents were more satisfied with their jobs when they met more often if they were dependent on the people with whom they were meeting to get their work done. However, attending more meetings was related to lower satisfaction if they were not interdependent. Respondents reported higher job satisfaction and well-being when they felt that the meetings were effective, regardless of how much time they spent in meetings or the number of meetings.

Another sample of 304 employees was asked about prescheduled meetings attended on the day they filled out the survey (reported by the same authors). The more meetings people attended during the day, the less they felt personally productive if they were high in their motivation to do well (accomplishment striving). However, the more meetings people attended, the more they felt personally productive if they were low in motivation to do well. In other words, people who really strived for personal achievement felt that meetings ate into their productivity. People who were less motivated apparently felt that meetings made them more productive, or at least made them feel more productive.

As a leader, make your meetings more valuable by focusing on topics and processes that involve all members and deal with their interdependencies. A meeting that simply reports independent efforts that have little to do with each other will do little more than convey information. There may be other ways to keep people informed than taking their time in a meeting. If meetings are scheduled at regular times, be sure agenda items do more than fill time, and deal with issues in which all or most members have a stake and activities that require members to work together.

Summary

In this chapter, we examined groups from individual, group, and organizational perspectives and as systems that evolve. We outlined common stages of group development, including what happens as the group evolves and what the leader does each step of the way. We noted that groups differ in how these stages unfold. We pointed out that many groups underestimate the time needed to complete their work and that groups often experience a midpoint transition, at first floundering and then, as their deadline approaches, coalescing around objectives and methods for achieving them. We described what we mean by group process, the meaning of group cohesiveness, and ways to facilitate group development. Here are the major points to remember:

- Groups operate on individual, group, and organizational levels. All three perspectives influence the process and outcome of groups in different ways. Individual variables refer to member behaviors and inclinations. Group variables are the interactions among the members and goals and outcome of the group as a whole. Organizational variables include sponsors, stakeholders, technology, and other aspects of the environment that impose expectations, pressures, and demands on the group. Sometimes contextual factors, such as the culture in which the group operates, have a powerful effect on groups. Sometimes the nature of the task and how the group is structured to work on the task are determining factors in what the group does. Sometimes leader and member characteristics and tendencies have a dominant influence on group process and outcomes. All three levels may be relevant in determining what you should do as a leader.

- Groups are dynamic systems. Members, who can be thought of as systems themselves, affect each other and the group. The group is a system, and it operates along with other groups in a larger system (the organizational system and environment beyond). Systems have input, throughput, output, and feedback components. They are dynamic, constantly changing and adapting to forces within and outside the group.

- Groups generally follow five stages of development: forming, storming, norming, performing, and adjourning. These are not fixed stages that always occur in this sequence. Groups evolve in different ways and may repeat the stages. As a leader, recognize these stages and periods of transition between stages, and consider what you can do to facilitate the process and take advantage of these transitions as learning opportunities.

- Learning occurs during transitions between stages—storming to norming, for example—when groups deal with unfamiliar situations and have time to establish new patterns of interaction rather than rely on existing patterns that may not suit an emerging need.

- Group members often underestimate the time required to complete a task, especially if they feel they have plenty of time available.

- Groups often flounder early on. They may not develop a definite focus, direction, and model of operating until the midpoint, when they realize they are running out of time. Floundering is not all bad. You may bring up new ideas and pathways that are the foundation for redirecting the group.

- Group process is a cycle of goals, interaction among members, outcomes, learning, new goals, and so forth. The leader and members engage in a cycle of comparisons, comparing outcomes to expectations and revising goals accordingly (London, 1982). Know where your group is in the cycle and what you have to do to move on. (See Chapter Four for more on this.)

- Periodically assess group progress. (We return to the important topic of assessment in Chapter Eight.) Tracking progress requires having clear timetables, assignments, and frequent communication.

- Assess group process. Are you promoting collaborative behavior, joint decision making, and information exchange?

- Ways to facilitate group development include describing expectations (yours as leader and the members'), outlining goals, listing what needs to be done, asking members to share similar experiences so they can learn from each other, determining whether the group has the resources it needs, establishing methods and measures, and implementing ways to stay on track, such as frequent communication.

Chapter 4

DETERMINING YOUR LEADERSHIP STYLE

What concerns do you have about leading a group? Should you maintain tight control or let the members call the shots? Suppose you're not a "rah-rah" kind of person, but your group needs to be motivated. What do you do? How much should you plan meetings ahead of time?

This chapter is about leadership roles and styles. Leadership is a balancing act. Leaders need to know how to balance three poles simultaneously: (1) group members' vested interests balanced with a common vision and goals that all members agree are important, (2) a tendency to control and direct the group balance with encouraging members to participate in the process, and (3) pressures for action balanced with time for reflection. We emphasize three leadership roles: communicating, building trust, and facilitating the group's process. We consider the difference between transaction-oriented and transformational roles and give you a way to assess what your group needs from you.

After reading this chapter, you will be able to:

- Know the three major roles of a group leader: how to communicate, build trust, and facilitate.
- Coach your group at different stages of group process, keeping in mind what the group needs most from you at each stage.
- Use the cycle of comparisons to track group progress.
- Challenge members and build trust to maintain their involvement.

- Be transactional and transformational depending on what the group needs.
- Set a positive mood.
- Assess and improve your style of leadership.

Defining Leadership Style

Leadership style refers to your behavioral tendencies, habits, or preferences. The term suggests that you have one way of doing things no matter what the situation is. Indeed, you may have behavioral tendencies that are part of your personality. However, you learn and try new behaviors all the time, and you have the capacity to vary your behavior to fit the situation.

Group success depends a lot on the leader's style, including the leader's ability to behave according to what the group needs. Clearly leaders shape their group's performance. Leaders of high-performing groups are able to persuade members to give up their selfish goals and adopt group or common goals and work for the benefit of the larger group. They help groups find resources. They also deal with uncooperative group members. These are just a few examples of how the leader can make life better for the group as a whole (Hogan & Kaiser, 2005). Nevertheless, leading a group is complex. Even if you know the group members well and understand the task at hand, you are inevitably working with people who have different levels of expertise, motivation, vested interests, and, of course, personalities. Also, there are likely to be a variety of external pressures—demands or expectations from a host of stakeholders and constituencies. There may be pressures to do things differently, apply new technology, or perhaps deal with issues of globalization. Members are likely to represent different functions or departments. They may have different cultural backgrounds and different perspectives, experiences, goals, and ways of thinking.

As we pointed out in Chapters One and Two, group characteristics, along with environmental factors and elements of the task and group interactions, affect how well a group will do. The design of the group task (goals, methods, and assessment), the time available, and whether the group members have the knowledge and skills needed for the task will determine whether your group will be high performing or whether it will struggle. Your style of leadership is another component that will determine the outcomes of your group.

Leadership style can have negative or positive components. Negative, or dysfunctional, behaviors may include the tendency to criticize people in public, make rude comments at another person's expense, ignore others' opinions, prevent others from speaking, or intimidate by creating fear of evaluation (for example, emphasizing that you are the one who evaluates their performance and implying an unfavorable personal outcome for members who do not cooperate). Positive, or functional, behaviors may include encouraging others to participate, allowing others to express their opinions, abiding by the group's decisions, and being welcoming and friendly.

Here, we help you understand alternative styles of leadership. As you read the chapter, consider your leadership strengths and weaknesses and how you challenge your group members to higher levels of performance.

Leadership as a Balancing Act

On the one hand, leaders can assert authority in an autocratic way. Their approach is, "It's my way or the highway!" They may provide clear direction, but they expect members to follow this direction blindly. On the other hand, leaders can empower group members to act by encouraging their participation in decision making and providing resources. Generally leaders need a balanced approach. After all, they want group members to be committed to the group's goals and involved in its activities. They also want to ensure that the group creates and achieves meaningful objectives. Consider the following three ways group leaders achieve balance:

- Balancing individual members' vested interests with working toward a common vision and shared goals. This means recognizing members' ideas and concerns while simultaneously unifying members around one or more common goals. Group members need to have a chance to express their individual concerns as well as discuss common goals. Eventually, with the hope that this is sooner than later, group members need to agree on what they are doing, why, and how.

- Balancing controlling the group with encouraging members to participate in the group process. Being authoritarian and directive may be easier for you, but if you want to draw on your members' knowledge and experience, you need to involve them in decision making. The importance of participation will depend on the value of members' contributions and the extent to which they need to be motivated to complete their work and coordinate their efforts to achieve group goals. Otherwise why have a committee or task force?

- Balancing spending time reflecting with pressures for taking action (Martin, 2006). As we point out in Chapters Seven and Eight, reflection is important to understanding group learning. Groups need to step back at various points, perhaps even after each meeting, to examine how well they are working together and how they can improve. Members and the leader may feel pressured to move ahead quickly and show progress, but without reflection, they may perpetuate ineffective behaviors, such as arguments, talking over each other, and not recording decisions.

Leaders balance three dualities: (1) individual vested interests versus goals that everyone in the group has in common, (2) control versus participation, and (3) taking action in response to external expectations versus helping the group to reflect on interactions among members. When a leader's attention is focused externally, trying to produce whatever the group is expected to do, the leader's attention is not focused internally. When the leader is controlling the group by providing directives, essentially telling people what to do, the leader is not being flexible or acting as a mentor, coach, or facilitator. Robert Quinn (1988), at the University of Michigan, developed the competing values framework of leadership to highlight two of these dualities: internal-external focus and control-participation (flexibility, to use Quinn's term). The model shows that these different leadership roles (directing attention internally or externally, and controlling or being flexible) are polar opposites. At least, leaders will have trouble working on both ends of each continuum (focusing internally and externally at once; controlling and being flexible simultaneously). The major components of Quinn's framework are outlined in Table 4.1

Table 4.1 Quinn's Competing Values Framework

Focus of Leader's Attention	Degree of Control	
	Control Oriented	Flexible
Internal	*Monitor:* managing collective performance, monitoring individual performance	*Mentor:* understanding yourself and others, being able to communicate effectively and develop followers
	Coordinator: being able to manage projects and design work processes	*Facilitator:* building teams, using participative decision making, and managing conflict
External	*Director:* being able to design and organize the group's work, including delegating effectively while being able to control where the group is going and plan how the group will get there; setting goals	*Broker:* being able to build and maintain a power base, present ideas, and negotiate agreement and commitment
	Producer: working productively and being able to manage time and stress while fostering a productive work environment	*Innovator:* being able to live with and create change and thinking creatively

Adapted from Quinn (1988).

Although the different roles may conflict, you do not necessarily have to do them all at once. You can learn to vary your behavior depending on what is needed at different times. Use the following checklist at the end of each meeting to see what you concentrated on during the meeting. For each continuum, what was the primary focus in the meeting? Or rate the extent to which you focused on each using a five-point scale from 1 = low to 5 = high:

Vested Interests–Common Goals

_____   Giving members time to express their individual concerns (vested interests)

_____   Talking about our common goals

Control-Participation

_____   Controlling the meeting

_____   Encouraging participation

Action-Reflection

_____   Taking action to respond to external expectations

_____   Talking about group process and relationships within the group

Over time, you will see the extent to which you are achieving a balance. You may be off-kilter, for instance, always worried about taking action and never taking time for group reflection. Or you might always encourage participation but do little controlling. In such cases, you can ask yourself (or your group) whether you should spend more time on the opposite end of the continuum. You might not have to, but then again, you might be able to help the group make more progress if you pay attention to balancing each of these three scales.

Situations and group processes are continuously in flux, and leaders need to be reflective and flexible. Maintaining balance is an ongoing process. Leaders always need to be cognizant of these balances and make adjustments. Sometimes the group may need to respond quickly. Indeed, there are times when the leader may need to make a decision quickly without achieving consensus, act without giving all members a chance for input, and maintain task focus without reflecting on process. However, in general, the leader needs to develop consensus around a common vision and goals, engage members in generating alternatives and making decisions, and facilitate process discussion and reflection. Think about these questions:

- How do I achieve balance between members' vested interests and gaining their commitment to a common vision?
- How do I achieve balance between directing and encouraging participation?
- How do I achieve balance between pressure to act and taking time for reflection about how we're doing and what we can do to improve?

Leader as Communicator

Now that we have considered leadership roles, let's think more about behaviors—what you actually do as a leader. In particular, we will focus on evaluating your group's progress and communicating with group members to make adjustments.

Leaders are constantly assessing group progress, comparing their accomplishments to their expectations, and redirecting the group to meet these expectations as the group process continues. In other words, leaders assess whether the group is accomplishing its objectives.

Leaders Compare Their Progress to What They Intended

Consider this study of thirty-four leaders of small groups who were videotaped in ninety-minute group sessions (Stockton, Morran, & Berardi, 2004). The leaders were asked to identify what they intended to accomplish at various points during the group discussion. The researchers did this by having the leaders observe tapes of their meetings. At regular intervals, the researchers stopped the tape and asked the leaders to write what their intentions were at that time. The study found a cyclical pattern of intentions and interactions that goes like this. The leader (1) attends to the group activity, (2) gathers information from the group discussion, (3) assesses the nature of the group dynamics including benefits and obstacles, (4) uses this information to guide and refocus the group, (5) observes the resulting group activity, (6) compares it with the result he or she has in mind as a finished product, and, coming full circle, (7) once again attends to the group activity.

As a leader, are you stepping back to consider how your group's activities are helping the group work toward its intended purpose and product? Are you stepping back to reflect on the group's discussions, examine the way members are working together, and identify obstacles that are hampering progress? If you do not, you may not be able to adjust the group's focus or shift its activities, for instance, at the midpoint transition from general information gathering and discussion to meeting a deadline. At any point, your group may need refocusing, but you will miss it if you do not force yourself, and indeed the group members as well, to talk about the group process.

The Importance of Effective Communication

When communicating expectations, giving feedback, and generating ideas for change, you can send a message in the form of a directive, an opinion, or information. But just because you deliver the message does not mean that your group members received it. A music analogy works well here once again. Consider the conductor who precipitously starts the piece without first making eye contact with the orchestra members and then giving a clear upbeat that indicates how fast he will take the tempo. The conductor might start, but the musicians might miss the first beat and not come in together, thus ruining the ensemble.

When you say something to your group members, maintain eye contact. Look at them, and wait for them to respond. If the room is quiet, let it stay quiet for a moment. Consider that the conductor is always present but is not the reason the music was written. Great conductors such as Leonard Bernstein may have been showmen, but they had to create great music. Audiences might enjoy watching a "dancing" conductor, but only if the orchestra produces a terrific, exciting concert. Similarly, good leaders do not overshadow their group. They bring out the best in each of the members and get out of the way so the group can shine. Moreover, group members must allow each other to shine and must not prevent their teammates from presenting their own ideas and using their skills to the fullest benefit of the group.

Consider the conductor who does not want to hurt anyone's feelings. He hears the flute is sharp, the second violins are not bowing together, and the cello is totally off the down beat. He knows these things, but he just says, "Let's try it again." He does not say why or give instruction about how to improve what is happening. Perhaps the players heard the problems and will correct them. Maybe they have no idea that these problems occurred and will do nothing to improve. Honesty and trust are important for valuable feedback. The players have to trust that the conductor hears well and will instruct them wisely. The conductor has to be honest and not personal in his corrections.

For another example, imagine a medical student who makes a mistake in a medical procedure and the supervising physician does not take the time to correct the student. Perhaps the physician wants to avoid confrontation. Is this student the future pediatrician you want to care for your children? Feedback is crucial in medical training, which often occurs in groups of students who are learning collaboratively. Clear objectives, together with a process for regular feedback, will help allay the awkwardness of giving negative feedback. In this case, the physician must be honest with the student, and the student must trust that the physician is giving the feedback in the spirit of helping the student and other students in the group improve, not to mention achieve the best outcome for the patient.

Generally group members must give each other respectful, behavior-based feedback to help the group move forward and change in positive ways. Members should not take the feedback personally but should seek feedback actively in order to improve the outcomes. Remember, too, that communication is a two-way street. Listening and asking for input are as important as stating your expectations.

Leadership Style and Feedback

Some leaders are comfortable with feedback and maintain positive channels of communication. Others are uncomfortable with feedback and create breakdowns in communication. Here are two examples of how leaders manage their work groups and how communication and feedback are part of their leadership style. The first is an example of a manager who is a poor communicator, and the second is an example of a strong communicator. As you read these examples, think about what these managers might be like as leaders of committees or task forces. Would you want them to lead a group you were in?

Example: Getting Enmeshed in a Bad Feedback Cycle

George is an upper-level administrator in a software development company. He spends most of his days in meetings with executives within the company and spends considerable time attending professional conferences to keep up with advances in the field. He is the chair of several task forces that are developing new software. Some of the people on these groups report directly to George. Others are from different departments in the company. Annually George needs to evaluate the performance of the people who work directly for him and provide information to the supervisors of others who are members of his software development teams. However, because George is away so often, he does not always know the extent to which each group member has contributed to each team effort. Occasionally he gives feedback to individual group members or to groups as a whole. His tendency in the formal and informal appraisals is to focus on negative events, things he is dissatisfied with, instead of painting a fuller picture of the person's performance and how he or she might advance or improve. Some of his workers wonder about the genuineness of these feedback sessions and why George does not take more time to discover what is really going on. George prides himself on his communication skills, which he thinks are good, and is unaware of the effect he has on the others in his work group.

Example: Creating a Good Feedback Cycle

Ann has a pleasant demeanor. With a cordial smile, she tours the office each morning, greeting everyone as she goes. She sometimes has a skewed sense of humor but is consistent in her expectations where work is concerned. She chairs several committees, and her committee members tend to trust her because she honestly admits when she makes a mistake and involves her committee members in generating clear goals and objectives. Ann is aware that the members of the groups she leads want and need feedback, and she offers it freely whenever an opportunity presents itself. Her demeanor when giving feedback is honest and sincere, even when it is uncomfortable. She gives the feedback in a confidential way and emphasizes formative feedback—information that will help the feedback recipient improve. Overall, she gets to know her committee members well. They confide in her and trust that she will keep what they say to herself.

So who would you prefer to lead your group: George or Ann?

Feedback and the Cycle of Comparisons

Good communication is often touted as an important, if not the most important, aspect of a successfully run organization. Feedback is a form of communication that can make or break a group. If it is clear, honest, and given in a way that encourages follow-up, it can strengthen a group and strengthen its communication cycles. But feedback that is contrived and not well thought out can be damaging and weaken ties between group members. Groups with strong communication that rely on well-thought-out, clear, and well-delivered feedback can create strong connections among group members.

Frequent feedback gives group members direction for how to proceed. Positive feedback lets them know they are on the right track. Negative feedback stops them from wasting valuable work time. If you give your members feedback about their behaviors (things they did that might have been more effective if done differently) and not their personalities (elements of their self-identity), they may be inclined to accept the negative feedback and may even ask for feedback. Negative feedback should be framed in a way that leads to positive results. It should be a learning experience.

Feedback Cycles. Start with a written statement of your group's mission. Ask everyone to read the mission, and let them ask questions to be sure they all understand it. Discuss what it is and what it means. Members may even help write and revise the mission and goals and may help develop more specific objectives. One member might have one idea, and another might have a different idea. They talk it out. This is a feedback circle in which they focus on the extent to which they agree on the mission and also on the importance of the mission. Now talk to the group's sponsor about the mission. The sponsor is your supervisor or the person who gave the directive to form the group, or to whom the group will report its results. Is the group's interpretation consistent with the sponsor's? Can the sponsor live with the group's interpretation, or is further discussion necessary?

Once the group, you as the leader, and the sponsor agree, the group begins the next cycle. They talk about what the next step is—for instance, who will do what, by when, how, and when they will meet to review what they have done. Again they discuss each question: What will be done? How? When? They agree and then move on. Sometimes they disagree. For example, group members might feel they are moving off track. They can consider alternatives. When they feel they have chosen the correct alternative, they move ahead to test whether it brings them closer to their mission. This cycle of comparing what you are doing with your expectation of the end point is essential for developing good teamwork. The group members are the sounding board. They let each other know when they are off track and need to be brought back into the circle.

Consider this general example. A group leader asks members to report what they have accomplished since the last meeting. The member who begins admits that she could not complete everything. The leader listens carefully and then asks the member what should happen now. The member hesitates, feeling she is being put on the spot, but then makes a suggestion. The leader asks other members for their reaction, and someone volunteers to help finish the work. The leader asks what could be done differently to avoid unnecessary work or move the group along faster. Members express their ideas, and the group formulates a strategy to solve the problem that was created because the member who was reporting did not finish what needed to be done. The leader then asks another member to give a report.

Let's look at some of the cycles that occurred in this scenario. First, the member giving the initial report had a goal. The leader accepted the member's explanation for not completing the work and asks for suggestions. The leader might also have asked why this happened and how it could be avoided in the future. Other members were asked for their constructive suggestions, including ideas for what could be done now and how they could help. This becomes an iterative process. Note that the leader does not blame the reporting member. The problem may have been the member's lack of commitment, a lack of resources, or an unpredictable occurrence that could not be avoided.

Continuous Feedback and the Circle of Trust.   Did you ever see the movie *Meet the Fockers?* The father-in-law develops what he calls a "circle of trust." The son-in-law has the task of remaining in the circle, as do other family members. The circle creates the tension throughout the movie until the family discovers that it is the father-in-law who is outside the circle and must come back in to rejoin the family team. Group members need to trust one another. Remaining in the circle should not be a cause for mistrust or tension between members. Members must trust one another to give solid feedback so that the circle is useful and functional. They should expect to fall out of the circle once in a while, and this might even be a good way to determine the boundaries of the circle. The boundaries define closeness to the mission. They might be defined by clear objectives that help members stay in the circle as they prepare a presentation, a project, or ongoing functions in an organization.

Here are some ways to accomplish this:

- Ask group members to assess your performance after each meeting or after every two or three meetings. Tell them they can do this anonymously by jotting some remarks on a paper or typing them up and leaving them for you in an envelope taped to your door, or giving them to your secretary, or having one member of the group collect them all and give them to you. Thank the group, and try to carefully consider what they say and make changes that seem beneficial.

- Between meetings, interact with group members individually to make a connection. Show you care about their contributions by following up after meetings to see that they understand their role and to ask if they need help you can provide. Offer positive feedback between meetings, and give encouragement. This shows group members that you are willing to take time just for them.

- Suggest that two group members work together on an assignment. Praise them for their participation to strengthen their bond with each other and with the group.

- Get to know each member, and create situations for members to get to know each other. Learning something personal about each other gives them insight into the people they are working with. They can socialize before and after meetings. Commitment to a group is stronger if members know each other personally.

- Spend time between meetings to summarize what was done during the meetings and what will be done between the meetings. Send session minutes to all members to remind them as well. Ask them to review the minutes before the next meeting and come with any questions they have.

- Encourage e-mail interactions between members so that they can share their research, findings, ideas, and writings before the next meeting. In this way, they have time to process the new information and bring richer concepts to the floor.

Feedback is an important element of the group assessment process. Appendix C offers ideas about how to give feedback to individual group members and to the group as a whole.

Building Trust

When group members trust each other, they let each other know their feelings, emotions, and reactions (Messina & Messina, 2006; Platts, 2003). They have and express confidence in and respect for each other. They are supportive and reinforcing, and they assume that they will not intentionally hurt each other emotionally if one of them makes a mistake. Leaders show trust in their group members when they reveal their problems, concerns, and mistakes. Essentially they place themselves in a vulnerable position, relying on the group members to treat them fairly, openly, and honestly

(Messina & Messina, 2006). Building trust requires being vulnerable, letting go of fear of others' reactions, and self-acceptance. People who have not been in a trusting environment or who were emotionally hurt when they expressed their feelings are likely to have difficulty developing trust. Also, people who are low in self-esteem are likely to feel they do not deserve others' expressions of concern and sincerity.

As a group leader, what can you do to build your group members' trust in you and in each other? Robert Sevier (2005), senior vice president at the marketing consulting firm Stamats Communications, observed that a leader can build trust in these ways:

- Articulate a few important goals.
- Meet commitments by doing what you say you are going to do.
- Insist on clear, important, and consistent goals.
- Be open, fair, and willing to listen (a trait that is important for all group members).
- Be decisive.
- Give credit.
- Respect the opinions of others.
- Empower group members to act (saying, "go ahead," and when they do, rewarding them, certainly not reprimanding them).

One way to develop trust and unite group members, particularly if they are a diverse and unlikely collaborators, is to present them with an irresistible challenge (McKenna & Maister, 2002). Challenges show the group members that you believe in them. The task itself can be a challenge, for instance, launching an exciting new information technology system or initiating a marketing campaign for a new brand. A challenge can be a high-profile project, a process improvement crusade, a tight deadline, or a chance to become the "winning underdogs." Lauren Keller Johnson (2005), at Harvard University, recommended that leaders create challenges in the following ways:

- Share as much information as possible.
- Provide the right amount of guidance (opportunities for participation balanced by guidelines for generating ideas and making decisions).
- Define success (creating a compelling vision).
- Clarify goals and direction.
- Take time to build trust (spend time together).
- Stretch group members beyond their current skills.
- Make the task fun, actionable, and visible, for example, designing a brainstorming session to mimic the TV series *The Apprentice*, in which Donald Trump challenges aspiring businesspeople and then "fires" mediocre performers (although we do not necessarily aspire to Trump's style of giving feedback).
- Help people feel the challenge (exercises that let your group feel the challenge viscerally, as when GM's Saturn division challenged retailer teams to brainstorm new ideas to "surprise and delight" customers).

We will say more about building trust in groups as this chapter continues. To move forward, think more broadly about how leaders can build trust and help the group accomplish its goals. This is transformational leadership.

Transactional and Transformational Leadership

Leaders engage members by making them feel they are part of the solution and maintaining their motivation. Contrast two leadership styles: transaction oriented and transformational (Bass, 1998). The transaction-oriented style formulates plans, organizes tasks, makes assignments, provides guidance and direction, monitors progress, makes decisions, and fixes any problems that arise. The transformational style creates and communicates a vision with members' involvement, empowers members to establish their own methods, makes decisions in line with the group's goals, and shares the leadership role.

Whether you are a transactional or transformational leader (or both) will depend on what you are comfortable doing and what the situation calls for. A transaction-oriented, directive, authoritarian style may be most productive when members do not have experience, do not need to be committed to the goal and task, and are likely to be minimally engaged in the effort. In such a case, they just need and want to be told where to be and when and what to do. A transformational, participative, democratic style may be most productive when members have considerable experience and knowledge, need to be committed to the goal (feel it is their own and identify with the work of the group, perhaps because the work requires a considerable commitment of time and energy), and are likely to care deeply about the effort, perhaps because of its significance to the organization or society or because of its visibility to others and its value for each member's career advancement. In such a case, members want to be respected, involved, and active in determining for themselves what they do, when, and how.

Your style will be a matter of personal inclination (what you feel comfortable doing), as well as a matter of assessing the situation and changing behavior to meet the needs of the situation. Use Exhibit 4.1 to describe your preferred leadership style and what you are willing to do if required by the situation. Fill in the boxes by checking those leadership behaviors you prefer and are willing to do. Also, for each type of behavior, describe what it is you like to do and believe you do well and what you are willing to do even if you don't especially like or feel comfortable with that behavior.

When should you be transactional and directive, and when should you be transformational and participative? This depends on need. Do members have information that can help the group, or do they have little experience that would not be helpful? Do members need to be committed to the work and the goals of the group, or can you simply assign them work and expect them to carry it out without a strong feeling of involvement? If the members have information that can guide the task or they need to own the task and goals

Exhibit 4.1 Assessing Your Leadership Style

Leadership Style	Your Personal Preference (What You Like to Do and You Believe You Do Well)	What You Are Willing to Do If Required by the Situation
Transactional Tasks		
Planning		
Delegating		
Organizing		
Providing direction		
Making decisions on your own		
Fixing problems		

Leadership Style	Your Personal Preference	What You Are Willing
Transformational Actions		
Envisioning goals and outcomes		
Fostering open discussion		
Involving others in transactions		
Involving others in decisions		
Empowering others to fix problems		

(that is, feel committed to them and identify with the group), then they should be involved in the process. The leader's role is to facilitate that process.

Think about a group you are or have been a part of and answer the following:

Did members have the capabilities to do the task?	Yes	No
Did members need to be committed to the work?	Yes	No
Would members be upset if you told them what to do?	Yes	No
Did members need to take responsibility for the final product?	Yes	No

If the answers were all yes, then a transformative, participative approach would be more effective than a transaction-oriented, autocratic approach.

Suppose the best strategy is participative, but you are a born autocrat who likes, indeed needs, to control situations, especially when you are in charge. Then this would not be a good group for you to lead, and you should consider bowing out of the leadership role if you cannot change your behavior and be more participative. If you want to try a more participative style and you are not comfortable with it, you might explain this to the group and ask for their thoughts along the way. Tell them that you want their feedback, and stop the group once in a while to ask for it. Also, alert the members that they should feel comfortable letting you know in public or in private when you are too bossy and controlling. Of course, this is easier said than done. If you need to maintain control, chances are you will not feel comfortable taking advice or getting feedback from others. Still, in the interest of your own leadership development, think about this carefully, and give it a try.

Does being a transformational leader really matter? Certainly a leader can have a powerful influence on what the group does and produces, but factors other than the leader can substitute for good leadership. Such substitutes include group members' abilities, members' professional orientation, their need for independence, the feedback they receive from doing the task, members' feelings of intrinsic satisfaction from working with the group, and the formality or clarity of the group's purpose and role in the organization. The performance of a group may be as much, if not more, a matter of substitutes for leadership than what the leader does (Jermier & Kerr, 1997).

Testing this notion, Robert T. Keller (2006) of the University of Houston examined the extent to which the substitutes for leadership and measures of leadership predict performance over one- and five-year time periods in groups engaged in research or product development. Two types of leadership were measured: (1) the leader's structure or control over what the group does and (2) the leader's use of communication and persuasion to convey a vision and generate commitment, called transformational or charismatic leadership. Transformational leadership was more important in groups engaged in research projects than development projects. Perhaps this is so because research projects are more ambiguous in what has to be done and how and what the end result will be, so a charismatic leader who is able to rally the troops and maintain the motivation may be especially important.

Shared Leadership

Transformational leaders share leadership roles. Although you may be the formal leader by virtue of your position (appointed or elected to the leadership role), as a transformational leader, you may be open to sharing leadership responsibilities with the group members. Collaborative leaders do not judge other members' ideas, and they submit their own ideas to the critical scrutiny of group members (Raelin, 2006). Moreover, when the leader is collaborative, group members believe that mutual inquiry may lead to something new or unique, or at least a different way of viewing reality. The group members become used to sharing information with each other, educating each other, and expecting members who have more knowledge or experience or are in a critical position to be more assertive (Pearsall & Ellis, 2006). Raelin (2006) outlined four forms of collaborative transformational leadership:

- *Concurrent leadership:* Group members recognize that there can be more than one leader operating at the same time. The formal leader willingly shares power with other members, and power can be increased when everyone works together.

- *Collective leadership:* Group members operate as leaders together. Leadership is a plural phenomenon; it does not stem from individual influence but from the process of people working together for a common purpose.

- *Mutual leadership:* All members are in control and may speak for the group, advocate a point of view to the larger organization or community on the group's behalf, and be assertive while remaining sensitive to the views and feelings of others.

- *Compassionate leadership:* The leader and the other group members are committed to preserving each other's dignity and valuing each member of the group regardless of his or her background, position in the organization, or social standing.

Sharing leadership may not be natural for you. Similarly, assuming some leadership responsibility may not be natural for the members of your group. It is not that they do not have leadership capabilities; rather, they are used to, and expect, the group leader to perform different roles and assume a higher level of responsibility than the group members. This may require some reflection and practice on both your part and the group's part.

The Leader as Facilitator and Coach

Sometimes groups work with professional facilitators who give advice to the leader and group members during the course of the group's work. Indeed, you may consider hiring a professional facilitator, or your organization may have facilitators on staff who help committees and work groups. We will describe the role and advantages of a professional facilitator later in this chapter and the next. Here, we recognize that as a leader, you can benefit from knowing and practicing facilitation skills. A good leader helps the group by establishing clear objectives (or, better yet, helping the group establish clear objectives), encouraging cooperation, and opening lines of communication and respect among members. The leader should be a good role model for other group members, showing them how to help (be a facilitator for) each other.

Consider what happens when this does not occur—when the leader fails to facilitate group process and is a model for negative behaviors. Let's say the leader attended other meetings that team members did not attend. Some of the actions taken by the other groups had effects on the group. The leader did not discriminate between important actions and unimportant actions. The leader started the group meetings with a report from the other groups and provided detailed information that occurred in the other meetings, most of which had nothing to do with the group's functioning. This added at least forty-five minutes to each group meeting. Group members were bored and angry at this waste of time.

Instead, the leader could have distributed a list of important points made at the other meetings, with decisions and actions highlighted for easy identification. The leader could have taken minutes from the other meetings and written them in a format that highlighted actions that were related to the group's functioning. All of the information could have been distributed to group members ahead of time so members could prepare questions about the information and not waste valuable meeting time on unnecessary material.

In another example, the leader sticks to the agenda no matter what. It is a good idea to have a clear agenda and stick to it, but there are exceptions. For instance, if you know that a member has to leave early but wants to weigh in on an important matter, you can change the order of the agenda items or plan to interrupt the meeting to give the member floor time.

Of course, leaders need to be sure that members meet their obligation to the group. Leaders can do that by working with the group to establish rules and policies. For instance, members who miss meetings cannot expect the group to change decisions made when they were not present. If, when they return, they insist that the group revisit decisions already made, this will slow the group's progress and frustrate other members. A strong leader will establish an attendance policy that requires that the group have a quorum of a certain number of members before having votes or making decisions. Members who do not attend or show up late must abide by the attending group's decisions.

The Skilled Facilitator

Facilitation is a learned skill. Indeed, sometimes you will do well to hire a professional facilitator who is experienced in group facilitation. A professional facilitator is intimately engaged in the group process while being detached from the outcomes. You should also recognize when and how a professional facilitator can help. You may need a facilitator to help establish how the group will operate and review the group's process and progress periodically with the group and with you alone. The facilitator can be a source of ideas and a sounding board for your concerns and ideas about the group. A meeting facilitator will work with you to organize and run the meetings, helping you build agendas and keep the group on task.

Roger Schwarz, an organizational psychologist who has written extensively about facilitation and change management, has outlined the components of facilitation (2002, 2005a, 2005b). He runs workshops to train consultants, coaches, trainers, and managers in facilitation skills. According to Schwarz, a skilled facilitator begins by developing a contract with the group leader that specifies the commitments of the facilitator and the group members, for example, specifying the duration of the consultation, agreeing to training sessions with group members on methods of group process such as brainstorming, and collecting and providing feedback to individual group members, the leader, and the group as a whole. The facilitator will determine methods for diagnosing the group's process, for instance, using periodic surveys and group discussion questions to identify the elements that make them effective and problems that reduce group effectiveness. He or she will likely engage members in discussions about the group's process and ways they can change how they work together. The facilitator may encourage group members to share the reasoning and intent underlying their statements, so group members do not make assumptions about each other and as a result increase their mutual trust. The idea is to help members understand the points of view of others in order to create trust, promote learning, and reduce defensiveness, particularly in difficult situations. Overall, the facilitator should be a role model for avoiding judging or blaming others, focusing instead on helping members appreciate all contributions.

Coaching

Coaching can take several forms. It can be helping members to acquire the know-how to contribute to the group, providing advice and feedback to individual members and the group as a whole, helping the group itself develop, that is, become better at what it does by facilitating interactions between members, clarifying and delegating (sometimes reassigning) work roles, and designing structures (subcommittee activities, delegating work assignments).

Coaches motivate group members, guide their task, and facilitate learning. Richard Hackman at Harvard and Ruth Wageman at Dartmouth described the role of the leader as coach (Hackman & Wageman, 2005). They noted that group leaders structure the team (for example, by selecting group members and making assignments), establish the group's purpose, arrange for the resources the team needs, remove organizational roadblocks, and coach group members. Coaching includes helping individual members strengthen their personal contributions to the group and working with the team as a whole to use its collective resources well. The type of coaching that works best depends on the stage of group process. At the beginning, the group members need to be motivated; they need to be convinced that their efforts will lead to success. At the midpoint, the group needs consultation to help them perform the task better. Once the task is completed, the group is ready to reflect on what they learned as individuals and as a group.

Coaching may be thought of as a branch of facilitation. Coaches encourage, motivate, and stimulate the group leader and members as well as help to facilitate to ensure that the group makes progress. According to Schwarz (2002, 2005a, 2005b), coaches create contracts for coaching work that make positive outcomes much more likely. They help groups make the changes they want by designing and using a variety of interventions, including role-playing and real-life experiments (behaviors group members can try). Leaders and managers can learn to be coaches. In Schwarz's workshops, participants learn to help people identify and attain their goals by clarifying and deepening the purpose of the coaching relationship. The coach learns to guide clients to success and fulfillment through interventions that encourage self-awareness. They learn to create clear roles, boundaries, guidelines, and goals with clients, both at the outset and during the coaching engagement, as a strong foundation for working together. They learn to identify critical issues and dilemmas with clients and jointly design ways to address them.

Culture, Climate, and Mood

To understand what we mean by a positive climate, think about the difference between a group's culture, climate, and mood. *Culture* refers to the values, attitudes, traditions, and expected and acceptable behaviors that characterize the group. These may stem from the group members' cultural background (for example, nationality) and the culture of the organization ("the way we do things" or "what we stand for around here"). A group may develop its own culture, adapting from the cultural context in which it operates.

That is, if the group is together long enough, the members may form their own traditions, values, and accepted behaviors—for example, "group members will not be late for a meeting."

Climate refers to how members feel about the group at any given time. Climate is variable and is a function of what is happening in the group. We may say that a group's climate is "cold" or "harsh" or, alternatively, that it is "warm" or "friendly."

Mood refers to emotions at a given time. Mood is not long lasting, although it may contribute to a prevailing climate. Mood is the feeling that members have at the moment. After a surprising announcement, we may say that the mood is "somber" or "gray" or that it is "upbeat" or "positive." Individual members' moods affect the mood of the group.

The leader's mood is the most influential in affecting others' moods, the climate of the group, and ultimately its culture. Like anyone else, leaders have bad days, and they have good days. As a leader, you cannot afford to turn off the positive energy of your group if you are having a bad day. Your mood will be contagious. If you are having a bad day, you might say something you will later regret, so think before you start the meeting. Concentrate on the task, not on the people and not on yourself. Focus on your goal.

Maintaining Consistency

Say a committee meets monthly. During the meetings, motions are made and voted on. There is always a quorum for the vote. However, not all members are present at each meeting. One month, a policy is voted in and put into effect. The next month, someone who was not at the first meeting and was absent for the vote but who has been on the committee for years complains that he never would have voted for that policy. Although there was a quorum and the majority voted the policy in, the group rediscusses the policy and ends up changing the vote to remove the policy that was just put in place. Two months later, someone else attends who had not realized that the policy was voted down. She brings up reasons that the policy should be back in place. No one remembers that the policy was voted in or how the history of the policy has played itself out. They promise to review the minutes for the next meeting, but they forget. Two months later, the issue is brought up again and the policy is voted in.

What steps would have saved this committee wasted time revisiting the policy at hand?

- Keeping minutes and e-mailing them to all members right after the meeting.

- Bringing a binder of minutes to each meeting so that past decisions can be looked up or cataloguing decisions for easy reference.

- Making a decision that as long as a quorum is present, the vote stands and that members must be present to vote.

- Making a decision that members do not have to be present to vote but they must vote within a certain amount of time after the minutes are distributed. Decisions are not final until that time passes.

Whatever the group decides, it has to have rules and stick with them. Otherwise, it will have difficulty building on past work accomplished. The leader should facilitate the creation by the group of a set of rules and not allow meandering during the meeting. This does not mean that bad decisions should be maintained or that changes should be avoided. Rather, it is that groups should be sufficiently organized so they do not waste time.

Although keeping track of discussions during meetings so that threads of discussions are recognized and remembered is important, actions should be recorded carefully. The leader should point out actions taken at past meetings when moving ahead on related threads. The leader offers the group consistency and a point of reference by doing this.

Respecting Group Members

Leaders need to recognize that group members have different personality characteristics and that if the group is to work well together, all group members must be respected for who they are and what they have to offer. Consider what happens when a leader fails to do this. As an example, think about a leader who has no patience when group members have trouble stating their thoughts clearly. The leader cuts them off when he loses his patience and says something like, "That's enough for now. Someone else?" The group member's feelings may be hurt or, worse, he or she may never speak at the meeting again or at other meetings where this leader is present for fear of being cut off. This would limit the member's ability to contribute to the group. The leader should consider that every member is a valuable player. Otherwise members' contributions may be limited to what the leader wants to hear.

So what could a leader do to deal with someone who goes on and on without getting to the point? Perhaps the leader might take the individual aside and say, "I notice you sometimes are uncomfortable at meetings, or at least it takes you time to put your thoughts into words. Your ideas are always valuable to the group, and I look forward to hearing them. Is there something I can do at meetings to help?" Or the leader can suggest that the member take a public speaking course or simply write down his or her ideas before speaking. The reality of the situation may be that some members need better group skills, and leaders can provide ongoing training and discuss performance improvements. This type of approach results in more positive relationships in the workplace.

Here is a checklist of behaviors that you might use in thinking about how you affect the mood, climate, and culture of the group:

Your mood: Are you . . .

☐ Relaxed?

☐ Moody or uncaring about individuals?

☐ Detached?

☐ Overly outgoing but insensitive to others?

☐ Uncommunicative?

Your consistency: Do you . . .

☐ Treat members differently?

☐ Act inconsistently in how you enforce policies?

☐ Never alter a rule of the group?

☐ Stick to the rules for the most part unless there is a good reason to do otherwise?

How you listen: Do you . . .

☐ Listen only as long as you hear what you like and then cut people off?

☐ Make suggestions and then listen to responses?

☐ Make suggestions but not allow dissension?

If others were filling out this checklist about you, would they check the same items? What other behaviors and categories would you add to this list?

Ideas for Your Leadership Development

To conclude this chapter, here are some ideas you might consider to understand and develop your leadership style:

List your strengths and weaknesses. Ask one or more colleagues (preferably people with whom you have worked before) to describe what they see as your strengths and weaknesses.

Think about what your group wants or needs from you. Stated another way, what are the key characteristics of your group that pose challenges for you as a leader? For example, is the committee large or diverse? Does it lack people with the needed knowledge and skills to help? Are resources tight? Are members likely to disagree or have limited time? Is the work thankless or unpleasant (for example, budget cutting that will lead to layoffs)? Given these demands and challenges, what does this group need from you? Someone who is thoughtful? Can involve others? Knows how to delegate? Is well organized? Communicates clearly?

List your key strengths. To what extent is each needed? What strengths do you need that you do not have?

List your key weaknesses. To what extent will each be a problem (because it is needed here or because it will create problems)? For example, you might have a tendency to avoid planning meetings and preparing agendas. This will be a problem given the complexity of this task, and so it is something you need to be disciplined about.

Keep a journal of your behaviors and actions in each group session. Note what new ideas you introduced, whether you talked more or listened more, whether you were able to keep ideas flowing, and whether there were times when you felt the discussions were going nowhere. Did you recap the last meeting's accomplishments and who had to do assignments for this week? Did everyone do their assignments? Why or why not? Did the group stay on task? Did you feel the group was moving in the right direction? If so, what did you do well to have this happen, or did other group members facilitate this? If not, what can you do better next time? Review your group's goal. Are you closer to reaching it? What can you change next time to improve the group's performance? Review your journal periodically to discern patterns of behaviors that you may wish to change. Highlight the behaviors, and monitor your changes.

Audiotape your group meetings (with the prior permission of your group members) and listen to parts of the tape after the meeting when you have time to consider what was said and done. Review how you interacted with group members, and see if there are ways you can improve.

Consider what is at stake if the group fails. How does the importance of the group's work affect your behavior? Does the pressure make you moody, demanding, anxious, and as a result disrespectful? Do some members of your group have more power than you do in other settings? (For instance, you are the leader here, but several higher-level executives are members of your group.) How does this affect your behavior? Does it intimidate you? Prevent you from being consistent? Do you give these executives more latitude than other members? Can you say no to them in the group?

Summary

Leading a group is a balancing act between competing pressures and demands. We emphasized three leadership roles: communicating, building trust, and facilitating. We distinguished between transaction-oriented leadership and transformational leadership and offered ways to assess your leadership style on these dimensions of leadership. What you do as a leader depends on what the group needs. A leader facilitates the group process and establishes a group culture. As you lead a group, be mindful of ways to become a more effective leader. In particular, keep the following points from this chapter in mind:

- Leadership is a balancing act in which you need to balance (1) fostering members' commitment to a common goal while recognizing that individual members may have their own vested interests, (2) maintaining control while encouraging member participation, and (3) responding to pressure to act and get something done while taking time for reflection about what is happening in the group and how the group might improve.

- The leader is a communicator. Leaders guide their group in relation to their expectations. This is a cycle of comparisons, examining group progress and outcomes in relation to expectations, and communicating clearly and often.

- Leaders need to challenge members and build trust to maintain their involvement. Leaders challenge members by asking them to work on important tasks that require their expertise.

Engaging tasks are fun and realistic. Leaders cause members to trust them and each other when they facilitate frequent and honest communication, articulate a few important goals, are willing to listen, and are fair. This is especially important when members are diverse, come from different backgrounds, and do not know each other well.

- The leader is a facilitator and coach. Coaching depends on what is needed. When the group begins, it is likely to need coaching that motivates members. When the group is in the midst of its task, it is likely to need help structuring and tracking the work. When the group is just about done, it needs to be rewarded and have time for feedback and process reflection.

- Groups need leaders who can be transaction oriented and transformational. Transaction-oriented leaders plan, organize, delegate, and coordinate. Transformational leaders involve members in creating a vision, articulating the vision clearly, and empowering members to establish their own methods and make decisions in line with the group's goals. Transformational leaders share the leadership role.

- Leaders set a positive mood and create a constructive climate in the group by maintaining consistency and respecting group members.

Part 2

TAKING THE LEAD

Chapter 5

GETTING OFF TO THE RIGHT START

This chapter explains how to introduce group members to each other, get members hooked on the group's mission, and create a group climate in which members feel comfortable. We give suggestions for introducing group members, establishing clear goals, and conducting the first few meetings. The start of the group is the time to set a climate in which members feel comfortable working with each other, which includes establishing some rules for how the group will operate. (See Appendix A for a quick start guide.)

After reading this chapter, you will be able to:

- Use the quick start guide (Appendix A) for getting your group off to a productive start.
- Plan your first set of meetings, including clarifying mission and objectives, establishing how the group will be run, putting members to work, and setting standards to assess group outcomes so everyone knows what to expect.
- Be sure members know each other's skills, abilities, and backgrounds and their strengths and weaknesses early in the group process.
- Identify and overcome barriers to effective group process that might arise during initial meetings.
- Promote collaboration and consensus.
- Be a role model for a constructive and psychologically safe group climate.
- Gain the credibility and respect of your members.

A Positive Beginning

Getting the group off to the right start is critical to avoiding barriers, overcoming them when they arise, and operating as a high-performance group. As a leader, you need to prepare for the first meeting by reviewing the purpose for the group, selecting the group members, considering potential problems and pitfalls, creating possible time lines, and thinking about how the group should operate. If you are working with a professional facilitator, plan to meet with that individual to review these issues. In addition, you might meet with several key group members, perhaps those who have experience in the group or with other similar groups, to consider alternative ways of running the group. Also, you should prepare the facilities for the first meeting: arranging for a room, perhaps ordering refreshments, and being sure that flip charts and computer equipment are available.

The first meeting should include introductions, emphasizing the value each member brings to the group. This is also a time when you can communicate a vision of what the final product might be like so all members have the same conception of what the group is trying to do. Alternatively, you might give the group a charge, and the group might brainstorm a vision of what the final product might be like. Once this is established, and recognizing that it might be revised later, the group can begin thinking about performance strategies: who will do what, when, and how. Generally the group is more likely to achieve its objectives if the members agree on what they are and how they will be assessed. Members should have a clear understanding of the task and its components and agree on a realistic time line and how they will measure their overall success. Of course, things may not go exactly as planned, but that is okay. Most groups make a transition sometime, reformulating their procedures and even their vision of what they are trying to do.

The first few meetings are the time to establish a climate of psychological safety in which members feel comfortable working with each other. This is when you set the foundation for how the group will operate.

Before reading this chapter, we suggest you review the quick start guide in Appendix A, which we hope will be helpful to you later as a reference whenever you begin to chair a new group or task force. This chapter provides more detail about how to get your group off to the right start and keep it on a positive trajectory.

Members' Early Motivation and Involvement

Once you form your group and members are getting to know each other, you can enhance the group's cohesiveness. As you move through the storming stage, you work through different conceptualizations of the group's purpose, goals, and outcomes. You are aiming toward a shared vision of what you are trying to accomplish. This refers to the extent to which members feel they are working toward a common goal, share viewpoints about how to accomplish the goal, respect one another, and rely on one another to get the group's work done—in other words, creating cohesiveness.

Example: Building a Cohesive Group

John Boulding, the leader of his church fundraising committee, was asked by the pastor to chair the annual fundraising dinner committee. The tasks were to choose honorees, advertise the event, send invitations, arrange catering and entertainment, and attend to the logistics needed to make the event successful. Success meant raising money, honoring the designated honorees (some of whom should be capable of contributing to the church and asking friends and colleagues to donate as well), and having a party. Some of the committee members had volunteered before the group started. John asked several acquaintances to be on the committee too.

The first meeting was disorganized and depressing for John, not to mention the members. The committee members had all worked together before on other congregation events (it was a fairly small community to begin with—about 125 families). One member

---

was disappointed that he was not asked by the pastor to chair the committee, and he said so directly. He had chaired the committee last year and felt that he knew what needed to be done. Ignoring this, John thought that the first thing the group needed to do was select the honorees. As soon as a member shouted out a suggested name, others chimed in to say why this was a bad idea. After two hours, the group had a list of possibilities that no one was happy with. The meeting ended with everyone disgruntled and John unclear as to whether he should ask some of the people mentioned as possible honorees or not.

So what went wrong? In this case, it is easy to be a Monday morning quarterback. Still, think about what you would do to avoid the mistakes John made. Apparently John did not plan the meeting beforehand. There was no agenda, and when people suggested ideas, the meeting became a disorganized free-for-all. Some members seemed to feel that they had to fight to get their ideas on the table. A more orderly process would have made it clear to everyone what they needed to do during the meeting and give them a common idea about how the meeting was going to progress. As an exercise, try writing an agenda John might have used.

Some suggestions to make your group as productive as possible follow.

Hand Out an Agenda

A committee meeting is not an open-ended get-together. It should be a leader-led, structured conversation with one or more goals in mind that follows a logical order and has intended outcomes. The leader should plan the first meeting. The agendas for subsequent group meetings will depend on what happens at the preceding meetings. The first meeting agenda should include: make introductions, describe the purpose for the committee, outline the parameters (expectations, resources, and constraints—for instance, "Our work must be complete within x months," or "We have x dollars to spend"), provide time for brainstorming and prioritizing suggestions, and make decisions on next steps.

Organize the Group

The leader might invite several members to be part of an executive subcommittee to help plan future meetings, review progress, chair meetings when the leader cannot be there, and take minutes. Formal, long-term groups such as clubs and boards will have people appointed or elected to serve these roles.

Review the Purpose, Intended Product, and Importance of the Task

Remind members what you all are trying to do and why this effort is important. Is the purpose to create a vision or strategy, improve a process, resolve an issue, or design and implement some activity? State the goals in clear terms—for example, "The goal is to raise between x and y dollars," or "The goal is to hold the event within the next four months."

Give All Members a Chance to Introduce Themselves

Invite members to talk about their past experiences with the task or special knowledge they bring to the table as new members. Members will perceive the value each person brings to the group. Also, members will be recognized and feel valued for what they have accomplished in the past and how they can help now. It is also a way for them to commit to the group task in public. Once they express a commitment, they are saying that they want to help make the group successful and they are likely to follow through on assignments or tasks they volunteer to do.

Start with an Icebreaker

An icebreaker is a way to get everyone to talk and feel comfortable. It might be part of the self-introductions or a separate activity. But remember that people often do not like cute, parlor game–like exercises that expose them in some way—for example, charades, or an exercise to find people in the group who have certain characteristics (same undergraduate major, same hobby, same occupation, same number of siblings), or for each member to provide an adjective that best describes him or her. People who are shy feel exposed and uncomfortable with these sorts of icebreakers, and people who are gregarious may feel that the exercise is a waste of time.

One icebreaker we have found to be surprisingly useful is to ask all members to tell the group a bit about their childhood, for example, where they grew up, how many siblings they had and whether they were the oldest or youngest, and where they went to college. This could be extended to mention something about their present life they are willing to share, such as marital status, number and ages of children, and town they live in. Although this is personal information and some people may not want to talk about it, especially in a business setting, it is fairly general cocktail party talk that most people do not mind sharing. Sometimes personal issues do arise that other members can relate to, such as illnesses or growing up in a single-parent home. Members may find things they have in common, and learning this information may make the group members more respectful of each other. They recognize that they all have trials and tribulations as well as reasons for joy, and it overcomes stereotypes or classifications people may have of each other based on appearance or first impressions. By the way, this does not have to be done at the start of the group, although that is a good time. It can be done anytime, particularly if the group seems to be bogged down, with some people not talking and others hogging the floor. It puts everyone on an even playing field and may encourage the more reticent members to speak up.

Another idea we mentioned above is to play a game where members have to find other members who have certain characteristics, such as mothers with the same name, born in the same month, or the same number of siblings. This works well with a large group of twenty or more. Members simply walk around the room and ask each other questions. The first person to complete the list wins a small prize (a company mug, for instance). For a more work-related icebreaker, you might create a business game that asks members to split into subgroups to perform a task, such as manufacture a cardboard boat. Provide a model and quality standards. Be sure to have plenty of materials. Offer a prize to the first group that designs and produces the most boats that meet the quality standards. Alternatively, play a board game such as Scrabble or Monopoly. Develop a trivia game with fun questions about your company or organization. Another idea is to take turns blindfolding members and have the blindfolded person follow the instructions of the group, for instance, to get through a maze of chairs.

Other ice breakers can take the group away from the organizational context and meeting to help members get to know and trust each other. You might have a dinner out without pressure to talk about the task. Just getting away and relaxing is a great way to get to know one another. Or arrange an outdoor experience such as skiing, hiking, boating, or fishing. Create a challenge where subgroups have to work together to accomplish a difficult task, such as building a hut. You can hire a company to arrange and facilitate this type of experience. Still another idea is to hold a retreat—a concentrated time away from the office to get to know one another (through icebreakers such as those above) and to get a start on the task. Getting away from the office and putting people in an environment that is new for everyone is a way to build a sense of community as members identify with the group. (For more icebreaker ideas, see West, 1999.)

Hold a Team-Building Event

A team-building exercise is an interactive experience that helps members get to know one another better and develop a sense of mutual trust. It could be a game, a field trip, or just sharing a meal. It could be run during a fifteen-minute break in the meeting, or it could be a half-day or longer event. Icebreakers are team-building experiences that happen at the start of the group. A team-building experience can also be held later in the group process, and may be especially valuable when the members are stuck on a problem or not reaching consensus on important issues.

Search on "team-building" on the Internet, and you will find numerous options, such as workshops on group dynamics topics (conflict resolution, negotiation, bullying, and prejudice in diverse groups are examples), business games, murder mysteries, wilderness challenges, sports events, motivational speakers, and resort trips, to name a few. What you do depends on the mood of the group and their time and patience. Having an engaging facilitator can be important, especially in dealing with recalcitrant members who are all too willing to spoil the fun.

The goals of a team-building exercise are to improve group process. Members should get to know each other better, realize the value that each person brings to the group, trust each other, feel they can be honest in expressing their emotions, and be willing to suggest ideas without fear of being evaluated. That's a tall order for any one event or activity. However, even a brief team-building exercise can move the group a step further in its development, making the members a bit more mature and able to handle pressures and unexpected problems.

As an initial team builder, try something that is inexpensive and engaging. For instance, split the group in two, and have the two subgroups compete in performing a task. Perhaps give them some materials and a prototype product (for instance, a homemade pinwheel), and say that the first group that produces ten flawless products gets to select where they go to dinner or will be served lunch by the losing group. After the exercise, spend some time processing what each group learned about their fellow members, what behaviors were barriers, and what they could have done to improve. Ask how these insights translate to the group members' abilities to collaborate with each other. Refer back to the experience when there are opportunities to apply these insights, for instance, as a reminder when a member blocks a decision or is argumentative.

If the group isn't in the mood for fun, a team builder can also be time away from the grind of the office to focus on the task. One group we know went to a conference of groups from other organizations that were engaged in a similar task. The groups met in plenary sessions and then had time to work alone for several concentrated periods. In between, they shared their progress with other groups and with a consultant. This three-day experience jump-started the group effort, helped the members get to know one another quickly, and made their meetings that much more productive when they returned home. Another committee started a project by attending a half-day meeting in a hotel conference room away from the office. This gave them time to focus on the project and get to know each other during breakfast, a coffee break, and lunch. The group got off to a rapid start and members felt their time was well spent.

Decide How to Decide

Have a discussion about alternative decision-making strategies. Discuss the meaning of consensus, methods for stating and seconding motions, and alternatives for voting, such as majority rule and two-thirds vote for choosing. Review how multivoting works as a method for prioritizing alternatives. Follow a consensus-building process to decide how to decide. For instance, ask members if they support a process of stating motions and majority voting. If some members do not support the proposed process, ask if they can live with it. Some may want a more stringent voting process, such as a two-thirds majority for making financial allocations. Work toward a solution that all members can support.

Brainstorm Ideas

Groups do not generate more ideas than individuals alone. Knowing this, when your group needs to come up with alternatives, consider asking individual members to generate their own ideas first. Then list the ideas with the group and ask members to generate more (West, 2002). Be sure to separate brainstorming from evaluation.

Use an organized method for brainstorming, for instance, start with a round-robin technique. Go around the room and let each person suggest an idea he or she thought of individually. People can pass if they do not have a suggestion, and you can return to them. Write each suggestion on a flip chart so everyone can see and read it (take care to write legibly, or let someone else who has better writing be the scribe). Do not let anyone evaluate the suggestions. This may take a strong hand because people will be tempted to say how they feel. Do not falter here by letting group members criticize others' suggestions. This will only prevent other members from making further suggestions.

Once all ideas are listed on the flip chart, take each suggestion separately and list the pros and cons for each. You might start a separate chart, list each suggestion one at a time and summarize the pros and cons on the chart as the discussion progresses. This is a way to keep the discussion on track and establish a pattern of cooperation. It will also help members trust each other. They will respect each others' ideas, giving all members a chance to make suggestions and express their views. In addition, by having all ideas on the chart first, you distance the discussion from the individual who suggested each item. The pros and cons then reflect how the item contributes to the group's goal rather than being evaluative of the person who offered the item.

Multivote to Prioritize Suggestions

Once the group has evaluated all the suggestions, ask the members to prioritize them. One way to do this is multivoting. Count up the number of suggestions and divide by three. This is the number of votes each person has. Ask the members to go up to the flip chart and put hash marks next to their top choices. They can put all their votes on one alternative or spread their votes out. Then count up the total number of points for each suggestion. The priorities will be clear. Members will not have to make a single choice, and there will be a clear outcome. Repeat the process in the case of ties.

Show Your Appreciation

Thank the members for their suggestions and views. Do this as you move through the discussion and at the end.

Ask for Volunteers and Delegate Work

The meeting does not end until you know what is going to happen next. You might ask members to volunteer for different tasks—for instance, "Priya, would you be able to . . ." or "Kent, you've done this before. Would you mind working with Priya to . . ."

Some Other Suggestions

Here are some other suggestions that might help get the group off to a good start:

- Provide food, especially if the meeting is likely to be long.
- If you want to get a lot done when time is of the essence, hold the meeting from 5:00 to 6:00 P.M. Have clear objectives for what needs to be accomplished, and do not provide food.
- Follow general guidelines for effective discussions: listen, ask for clarification, manage participation, manage time, close discussions, stop digressions, and manage disagreements.
- Develop a schedule or chart that shows who does what and when. This is a way to hold people accountable for their commitments.
- Be sure someone is taking minutes and posting or distributing them so all group members, even those who must miss the meeting, know what occurred. Minutes should be accurate, clearly written, distributed to all members, and archived for

future reference. Reading them at each meeting will help pro-vide continuity of thought and action.

- Use a Web site to host an electronic group portfolio where members of the group can post their work, comment on each other's drafts, make suggestions, make changes to products, and have online meetings. In work settings, group members can use the Web site to maintain samples of the work they did in groups so their supervisor can review them during their annual performance appraisal.

Why Introductions Are So Important

Of course, you will begin the group by having members introduce themselves. This seems to be an obvious thing to do, but in fact this step is often incomplete. Certainly members state their names and their departments, but this says little about how they might con-tribute to the group. Their demographic characteristics—age, gen-der, race—will be evident and point to the diversity of the group, at least as far as these individual characteristics are concerned. These demographic characteristics probably have little to do with the committee's or task force's work since they do not provide informa-tion about members' skills and knowledge. Nevertheless, demo-graphic characteristics may be relevant. Perhaps the task has to do with being sensitive to different ethnic or age groups. The charac-teristics also may invoke stereotypes about what members expect from each other, whether these are valid judgments or unjust biases.

The Importance of Introducing Group Members to Each Other

Jeffrey Polzer, a researcher at the Harvard Business School, and his colleagues William Swann at the University of Texas at Austin and Laurie Milton at the University of Calgary showed the importance of group introductions within the first ten minutes to later performance (Polzer, Swann, & Milton, 2002). Groups in which members saw each other similarly and knew how each member could contribute to the group were more effective than those that did not. This was especially true in diverse groups in which different types of backgrounds and expertise were important to developing creative solutions. Polzer and his colleagues studied 423 business graduate students in their first semester. They were assigned to 83 study groups with 4 to 6 members per group. Groups were formed to be diverse in gender, ethnicity, country of origin, previous job experience, and proposed functional concentration in the M.B.A. program. During the semester, they completed various group assignments. Groups in which members shared information about themselves early during the first group meeting and gave each other feedback about what they heard developed a similar view of each other and performed better throughout the semester, especially if the group was diverse. If the group failed to share information about themselves and members did not see each other similarly, diversity hampered the group's performance. Apparently the diversity limited group members' ability to interact and cooperate with each other unless they could see how the diversity could help the group. Sharing information and giving each other feedback so that members saw each other similarly and in the same way that members saw themselves helped diverse groups to take advantage of this diversity to generate more creative solutions.

Introductions are important to get beyond misguided but perhaps long-held biases and help members gain an understanding of the ways each member might contribute to the group. They should let people know about their functional and educational backgrounds—the activities and experiences that are relevant to helping the group accomplish its goals. They should also let people know something about themselves personally—perhaps their family history or current family situation, or they may share a difficult experience they have had in their lives that required them to overcome some barrier. This sharing of information gives members a common ground and basis for perceiving each other's vulnerabilities. As members get to know each other, they express their strengths and weaknesses in an honest way and ask for feedback to be sure that other members heard them and to validate their self-perceptions (for example, "How do you think I can help this group?").

Some people use these early introductions to give other members a positive opinion of themselves to boost their self-image. However, most people do not do that. Instead, they want their fellow group members to have an accurate impression of them. They do not want them to think they can do more than they actually can do or that they know more than they actually do. They want them to have an accurate reflection of their abilities and knowledge, both their strengths and their weaknesses. Leaders can facilitate this process of introductions by asking members to share information about themselves.

Developing Collective Memory

When members learn about each other's roles early in the group process, they develop confidence in each other and have enough understanding of the contribution each person can make to the group. Cross-training in task roles helps them communicate with each other. They also develop more confidence in who can do what. They can still specialize in their individual roles.

Developing a Memory for Who Does What

Groups develop routines for handling tasks. These routines are useful when the group is assigned a new task similar to one they did in the past. Essentially the group prepares for, and may even rehearse, how to work together. This applies especially to groups that are in operation for awhile and may stay intact long enough to handle several projects. A simple example may be the committee that plans the annual holiday party for the office. The committee might start meeting in October and finish when the party is held sometime in December. If the same people come together again to plan the party the following year, they have a system that they can repeat. They know who did what and what worked well and what did not. They may make some adjustments, and of course, some new people join the group. Each year, the committee becomes more adept at planning the party, and the task becomes a bit easier. Group members develop a collective memory of their expertise, credibility, and coordinated interactions. This is sometimes called a transactive memory, referring to recollections of the group's transactions.

Over time, group members learn who in the group is best for doing what. Members specialize in different areas, usually based on their strengths and what they like to do. They learn this and rely on one another to be responsible for this expertise. Each member can then take the time to concentrate on and become better in using their area of specialized skill or knowledge. The awareness of each member's special abilities facilitates quick and coordinated action and access to deep, specialized knowledge when needed. Elements of this memory of group transactions include (1) *specialization* (each member has specialized knowledge of some aspect of the project), (2) *credibility* (the members trust other group members' knowledge about a project and have confidence in relying on information that other group members bring to the discussion and not needing to double-check information), (3) *coordination* (group members work together in a well-coordinated way and have few misunderstandings about what each other does in the group) (Lewis, 2003; Wegner, 1987).

Group Members Learn About Each Other's Expertise, and This Helps the Group's Later Performance

Kyle Lewis (2003) at the University of Texas at Austin developed the concept of the emergence and value of a group's developing a transactive memory system—an understanding of the differing expertise, credibility, and coordination of group members (Lewis, 2003). Transactive or collective memory is especially important for tasks that require a range of expertise that no one member is likely to have and members need to trust that other members' knowledge is credible and group members can work together in a coordinated way. Developing an understanding of each member's expertise and ability to work together early during the group helps members plan the task, break it down into discrete activities, and match members to these tasks. As the task progresses and members communicate with each other, particularly if they communicate frequently face to face, the transactive memory matures. Studying sixty-four M.B.A. consulting groups, most with four members each, Lewis (2004) found that a stronger transactive memory system emerges when the group members have different expertise, they know each other fairly well prior to the start of the group, and they communicate frequently. Groups perform better when they develop this memory of each person's expertise early, during the planning phase. This is consistent with the research of Polzer et al. (2002), described earlier in this chapter, indicating that groups perform better when members introduce themselves early in the group process and verify each other's expertise.

Each group member develops his or her own memory of the group members' expertise and interactions. Members' unique contributions to the group may be recorded in the group's minutes, but for the most part, this information is already in members' minds. As such, members may have somewhat different views of each other's abilities, interests, and relationships. However, this memory has value when members have similar views of each other. This becomes a collective memory and gets tested when the group is asked to do something new. The collective memory works well when the new task is similar to the earlier tasks, and members have similar recollections. The longer the group is in operation and the more it repeats similar tasks, the stronger the collective memory is likely to be. Short-term groups develop transactive memories quickly. They may not have a chance to use these memories again, or they may, as when members join other groups with some of the same members and draw on their memories of people with whom they have interacted in the past.

Consider a committee of community members who are coming up with designs for a new town hall square. Perhaps some of them worked with each other on the development of the town's community center that was built the previous year. Jeff may be remembered as an architect in the community who worked closely with the professionals hired by the group to monitor the quality of their work. Song-yee may be remembered as a long-term resident who knows many other people and has her finger on the pulse of the community. Members learned they can rely on Song-yee for having accurate information about differences of opinion in the community. Ian, an accountant, may be remembered for his financial expertise and his ability to work cooperatively with others.

Assessing Your Group's Collective Memory

To find out whether your group has a clear collective memory, consider whether these characteristics apply to your group (adapted from Lewis, 2003, 2004):

In my group . . . (check all that apply):

Specialization

☐ Each member has specialized knowledge that is important to our work.

☐ Different group members are responsible for expertise in different areas.

☐ Our work requires the specialized knowledge of several group members.

Credibility

☐ I trust my group members' knowledge and expertise.

☐ I am confident relying on the information group members raise.

☐ I have no need to double-check facts and figures group members provide.

☐ I have faith in group members' expertise.

Coordination

☐ Our group members work together in a well-coordinated way.

☐ We rarely misunderstand about what we need to do.

☐ We accomplish our work smoothly and efficiently.

☐ We rely on each other to get our work done.

Cross-Training

Collective memory suggests that group members get to know each other's skills and knowledge over time and rely on each other to develop and apply these skills and knowledge when needed. A related line of thinking suggests that group members should learn each other's role early on in the group process. This is called *cross-training*. Members do not have to learn all the roles and skills, just enough to understand them and see how the members can work together effectively.

The Value of Early Cross-Training

Cross-training helps members understand each other's roles. Members shift from specializing in their own roles to understanding each other's roles well. Researchers studied thirty-six three-person groups of college students who worked together on a task for four hours (Cooke et al., 2003). The task was a simulated helicopter rescue-and-relief mission that required extensive pre-mission briefing and planning and various aspects of group knowledge, such as communication, awareness of the situation, and sharing knowledge. Each group member received information about a specific role, such as pilot, intelligence officer, or navigation officer. Missions varied in objectives, such as to rescue civilians versus dropping supplies at a specific location. In one condition, group members were trained in their specific roles. In the cross-training condition, each participant received training for all three roles. Members of cross-trained groups had more knowledge of each role and the specific information that members in different roles had to pass to one another (a measure of teamwork). The more task and group knowledge members had, the better the groups performed. Higher-scoring groups had more accurate knowledge, and group knowledge accuracy improved over time as the group members interacted. This research suggests that cross-training in different roles at the start of a group can increase the extent to which members share and understand information about specific problems as the task unfolds. The implication is that sharing information about roles early in the group process is beneficial to later effectiveness.

Other research suggests that the intensity or depth of cross-training depends on the extent to which the group members need to interact interdependently. If the work requires close coordination, such as sequencing and timing of action, group members should have a more intense form of cross-training that provides examples of how members in different roles should behave (for example, videotapes that show models of role behavior so they can observe the functions of each role rather than just hear about them). If the task allows members to work independently, then observing models of behavior is not necessary (Marks, Sabella, Burke, & Zaccaro, 2002).

Leadership Challenges for Getting the Group Moving

Getting the group off to the right start and progressing smoothly toward goal accomplishment is not necessarily a smooth process. Some barriers are likely along the way. Here, we consider some of the barriers you might experience early on and what you as the leader can do about them.

- You have trouble finding a time when all group members can be present.

    Set a regular meeting time (the same time and day each week) when most members can attend.

    Set meetings on different days and times, and do not expect everyone to attend all the meetings.

- The directives for your project might be sketchy at best, and you do not have enough information to know exactly what is expected of you.

    Meet with the person who gave you the directive, and try to get more information.

    If this is unsuccessful, invite the person who gave the directive to attend one of your meetings to talk about his or her expectations.

    Attend meetings of other groups working on parallel projects to see how they are doing the work.

    Talk to other group leaders to see how they handled similar situations.

    Best alternative: Communicate so you get information that helps you move on.

- This is your first time as a group leader, and you're not sure where to begin.

    Follow the quick start guide in Appendix A.

- You do not know your group members, so you do not know what they can do and what their experience is.

Explore members' backgrounds as they introduce themselves at the first meeting. That way, all members will
have an accurate view of what they can expect from
each other. Generally people want others to see their
strengths and weaknesses accurately; they do not want
their fellow group members to have expectations they
cannot live up to.

- You tend to be talkative and are afraid you will not be a good
listener or that group members will not want to hear what you
have to say.

     Ask a group member you know well to be watching for
     this and give you some feedback after meetings.

     If you are working with a facilitator, let the facilitator know
     your concern and ask for some feedback and coaching.

- You have trouble talking in front of groups.
- A facilitator or trusted group member can give you some help.

     This might require just practice by doing. You will feel
     more comfortable as you gain experience.

     You need resources to complete the project and are not
     sure they will be available when you need them.

     Ask your supervisor or sponsor about this concern. You
     and the other group members do not want to waste your
     time if there is no hope of obtaining the resources you need.

     Consider ways to reduce needed resources, for example,
     be more efficient to do more with less, or change how
     you will achieve your objective, or perhaps the objective
     itself, to be in line with available resources.

- Your group strays from the directive you have been given and
morale is low. How do you pull them back on track?

     Ask the group to step back and talk about their percep-
     tions of what is happening and how they are feeling.

- Your supervisor criticizes your style but provides no clear feedback on how to change.

>Do not let your supervisor get away with this. Ask for a
>private meeting to talk through the issues.

- Your supervisor attends one of your meetings and rudely interrupts your agenda, saying that the group's progress is less than
stellar. By interrupting the discussions repeatedly, he prevents
you from completing your agenda and you find that you have
to start over again with only half the time left to complete
your project.

>Resign as the group leader, or ask someone else in the
>group to help you out.

>Ask the group members what they think and how they
>think the group should proceed.

>Meet with the supervisor, and say how you feel. Ask for
>more specific feedback and help. This is what we recom-
>mend, but other leaders might do it differently. This will
>depend on your stability in the organization, your self-
>esteem, and your ability to deal with adversity should
>your noncompliance come up again at a future meeting
>or when the project is completed and presented.

- Incentive systems in your organization reward individual
rather than collective accomplishment.

>Create incentives for group achievement that everyone
>will want to work toward. Competitions between groups
>sometimes work. Simple rewards, such as a party for the
>group, might also be an incentive. Generally emphasize
>what the group as a whole has to gain and how each indi-
>vidual will benefit from being a member of, and identified
>with, a successful group.

- There is a mistrust among group members of people with different backgrounds, levels of education, functions, departments, and territoriality—people protecting their turf, for
instance, or members with a particular expertise or from a
particular function conveying directly or indirectly that only
they can do a particular task.

Raise these issues with the group. Try to deal with them directly.

If necessary, take members aside privately to talk about their feelings and behaviors toward each other.

Creating a Climate of Psychological Safety

In a psychologically safe environment, members:

- Respect each other's abilities
- Are interested in each other as people
- Are not rejected for being themselves and stating what they think
- Believe that other members have positive intentions

Psychological Safety and Trust

Amy Edmondson (1999) at the Harvard Business School studied fifty-one work teams in a manufacturing company. She defined psychological safety in a group as members feeling that they can take a risk with the others. For instance, they feel free to suggest a new idea, express a controversial opinion, or disagree with others. Edmondson found that committees and task forces that have a climate of psychological safety are more likely to learn than teams that do not, and learning improves the effectiveness of the group. In teams with psychological safety, members trust one another (that is, they believe that they have each other's interests in mind) and respect one another so that they are comfortable being themselves. Group learning is an ongoing process of reflection and action.

It is characterized by members asking questions, seeking feedback, experimenting, thinking about the results, and discussing errors or unexpected outcomes of actions. Team members discover limitations in team plans when they test assumptions and raise differences of opinion openly, so they need a culture of trust and safety to learn. Edmondson found that psychological safety stems from a supportive interpersonal environment and a supervisor who coaches the team, respects fellow members, and gives people the opportunity and thanks for expressing their opinions.

The icebreakers we described earlier in this chapter are a way to begin building a sense of psychological safety as members get to know one another. Clearly, though, this is an ongoing process. Members gain respect for and trust in each other as they participate actively in group meetings, show their interest and concern in the group's goals, and make and meet commitments. Group leaders help create a climate of psychological safety by being honest and open, following through on commitments, encouraging members to participate actively, and abiding by decisions made by the group through consensus or voting.

The Leader as Role Model in Creating a Positive Climate

During the early phases of the group process, especially the first several meetings, you as the group leader can be a model for compromise and collaboration. You might explain these different methods of conflict resolution, give some examples, and ask members if they can agree on a collaborative model. (Appendix B has useful hints about how to negotiate and resolve conflicts.)

Most of us know ways to avoid making others defensive and generally to create a positive atmosphere. Of course, this is easier said than done, since what we say and do is often influenced by our emotions and the reactions of others to the situation. Remember that we choose our own reactions. As a leader, be mindful of your behavior and the effects you have on your group members.

Dealing with Disruptive Members

One or more members can disrupt a group discussion in several ways. A meeting can get off on a tangent or be overtaken by a member who monopolizes the conversation. Although an assertive member can make the group more effective if that person is in a critical position or has critical knowledge (Pearsall & Ellis, 2006), an assertive member can also waste a lot of the group's time and prevent progress. Assertive members or leaders can also be rude and curtail discussions by bullying members into taking their positions. People are hard to control, especially in groups of volunteers. Also, some members may not care about, or be sensitive to, the needs of other group members or the goals of the group as a whole. So when they have an idea, they get it out on the table, sometimes at inappropriate times. For instance, you may be addressing an agenda item that deals with analysis of expenses, and someone wants to express an idea for attracting more revenue. This comment leads others to discuss the merits of the idea or express their own ideas for revenue generation, when this was covered at the last meeting or is simply irrelevant to the current discussion.

One method for handling such a situation is to have a blank flip chart page ready at the start of each meeting. Label this, "Ideas to Discuss Later." When a tangential point is raised, stop the speaker, say that this is something the group needs to come back to but is not the topic under discussion now, and jot a note on the flip chart to describe the point so that you and the group will remember it later. Include a section on ideas for discussion in the minutes to be sure you do not forget the item and give the contributor the respect for raising the point.

Other ideas for handling disruptive members include the following:

- Take the member aside after the meeting and explain ways that you believe he or she could make a more valuable contribution. If this hint doesn't work, review the events of the meeting with the member, and together reflect on how the member got the group off track. Remind the recalcitrant group member about the value of having a positive reputation as a person who makes constructive contributions to group efforts.

- At the end of a meeting, or midway through it, say, after a five-minute break, lead the group through a process discussion. Ask them whether their discussion was productive and what barriers there were to moving ahead. Let members give each other feedback, and let peer pressure take its course.

- Be sure your minutes are attuned to highlighting actions that the group has taken. Discussions should revolve around motions, and actions should be the results of motions. If your group knows that they have to stick to the motion and have the responsibility of coming up with an action, they may help you, as leader, keep everyone on track.

- Impose a structure for discussion. For instance, when a contentious point of discussion is raised and many members want to express their views, allow each person to speak in turn for two minutes, and monitor the time limit closely.

- Bring something unusual and fun to the meeting, such as a wand, stuffed animal, or puppet. When things get out of hand, determine that only the person holding the object can speak and only about the motion on the table. Members will laugh because they have to hold the object—but they will also clamber for it to express their ideas.

- If all else fails, change the group's membership.

We say more about how to deal with difficult group members in Chapter Six.

Gaining Credibility and Respect as a Leader

Group members can immediately tell whether you are knowledgeable about the issue at hand. Be honest. If you do not know about the subject under discussion, do not say that you do. Let the group know that you depend on them as much as they are looking to you for answers. Here are some ways to handle this situation and lead the group in general:

- Start by discussing what the group members know about the problem or project at hand and how they can contribute to the group. This will give you an idea of what group members already know. Listen and take notes regarding the strengths and weaknesses they bring to the group: their skills, experience, attitudes, and knowledge.

- Ask the group members to spend a few minutes on their own writing statements of group objectives. Then have them share them with the group. Put them on a flip chart (or, if this is a virtual group, list them on an online bulletin board). Then ask the group to discuss them and reach consensus around a single statement.

- Brainstorm ideas for achieving the group's objective. List as many ideas as possible; synthesize them to remove redundant ideas. Then use multivoting to select the most feasible or well-liked possibilities. Vote on the final list using majority rule to make a selection.

- Set up group rules. Will the meetings start on time even if a few members are not yet there? Will members commit to being on time? Will they commit to completing assignments on time or letting other members know who can help so that the work gets done even if the person gets derailed on another project temporarily? Will meetings be held during work hours or on weekends and evenings? Establish rules of order—for example, not to talk about or criticize members when they are not present; respect members' other work and family responsibilities; agree to maintain commitments and hold people accountable; agree on how many meetings may be missed before being asked to leave the group; and agree never to be late for a meeting.

- Give group members resources and assignments so that they also become experts on the issues at hand. The more they know, the richer your results can be.

- Do not compete with group members. Allow them time to speak and give their ideas. Do not cut them off unnecessarily; a curt cutoff conveys the message that you do not value their ideas and that they may be sanctioned in the future for saying something they think is important.

- Ask individuals to assume different roles for each meeting or for the duration of the group—for example, elect or appoint a secretary, who will take minutes, or a scribe to jot down ideas on a flip chart. Clarify roles: leader, members, facilitator, and sponsors. Ask members to identify those who hold these roles, what they should do, and what they expect them to do.

- Describe how delegation and accountability will work, for instance, that you will make project assignments along the way and that subcommittees need to submit reports before each meeting.

- Avoid rehashing subcommittee work. Review their recommendations and rationale, and refine and vote or agree to adopt recommendations. Or send the subcommittee back to work with new suggestions and recommendations based on their reports.

- Have an action plan for communication, acceptance, and gaining commitment.

Summary

This chapter focused on getting a group started and moving in a positive direction. We covered ways to generate and maintain members' motivation and involvement from the start. We emphasized the importance of members getting to know one another well, especially gaining an accurate understanding of the value each person brings to the group. The chapter considered ways to create psychological safety. We also addressed ways you can gain credibility and respect as a leader. We leave you with the following suggestions and points to remember:

- Use the quick start guide (Appendix A) whenever you begin to lead a new committee or task force.
- Draw on a variety of methods for facilitating group dynamics, such as brainstorming, multivoting to prioritize, showing your appreciation, and asking for volunteers.
- Self-introductions are a way for members to explain to each other how they may contribute to the group. Introductions and icebreakers can establish psychological safety early in the group process.
- Use teambuilding exercises as a refresher later in the group process to provide some distance between tough issues, especially when there is considerable disagreement and a need to focus on common goals.
- Be open and clear. Communicate frequently, and ask others what they think.
- Create incentives for group participation so that members will want the group to succeed.
- Gain credibility and respect by listening and involving members (requesting and valuing their input) while conveying a vision. Members who care about an issue and are respectful of each other are likely to collaborate effectively.

Chapter 6

WORKING SMART

This chapter will help you solve some common problems to make your group as effective as it can be. For instance, you might ask, What if I can't get someone to stop talking? What if disagreements lead to antagonism (personal attacks such as name-calling)? In meetings, should I be flexible or stick to the agenda? How do I get help organizing and planning for meetings? What if a member interrupts the agenda and pulls the group off course? What do I do if people stop coming to meetings? What if we keep talking and planning but cannot arrive at a decision? What if we make a decision but no one volunteers to implement the decision?

In this chapter, we show you how to improve the way the group functions. We look at group performance at different stages of development. In particular, we address what you need to think about as the group is getting started (the forming, storming, and norming stages described in Chapter Three). We talk about how to find help—people who can give you advice or work with the group directly to facilitate meetings. Once the group gets down to doing its work, we show you how to keep everyone moving, increase cooperation, reach consensus, and deal with problem members. As groups continue to work on a task, conflicts may arise, and the group cycles through another storming stage. We show you how to nip these conflicts in the bud rather than ignore them and let problems fester. Finally, we describe how to give feedback to individual members and the group as a whole as the group winds up its business and members are open to reflecting on their experience. The chapter will help you motivate your group members, increase their enthusiasm for the group's work, and encourage them to attend group meetings and participate actively. To provide further guidance, we offer some strategies for negotiation and conflict resolution in Appendix B.

When you finish reading this chapter, you will be able to:

- Keep members focused on achieving the group's objectives.
- Follow structured steps to run a quality improvement team.
- Help your group members feel positive about the group's ability to accomplish its work.
- Build positive relationships among group members.
- Plan to integrate input from different members who are working interdependently.
- Delegate work.
- Hold members accountable for meeting their commitments to the group.

Group Effectiveness

Your job as leader is to do all you can to make the group effective. You may have the components of a high-performing group (the right people, clear goals, and the time and resources you need), but can you maintain it and produce high-quality work? Effectiveness means, first of all, accomplishing the group's objectives. It also means doing so in ways that make this a positive experience for the group members. How can you keep people motivated and the discussion on track? How can you be sure the group will finish its work on time? How can you involve everyone, taking advantage of each person's expertise and willingness to contribute? What can you do when people argue, come to meetings sporadically, or seem unable to make a decision or follow through to carry out a decision? Suppose meetings drag on with little accomplished?

In his book, *The Five Dysfunctions of a Team* (2002), Patrick Lencioni identifies typical dysfunctions or weaknesses of groups: (1) letting status or ego get in the way of producing results, (2) having low standards and avoiding accountability, (3) causing confusion and ambiguity because group members lack commitment and dedication, (4) creating a sense of artificial harmony to mask a fear of conflict, and (5) not taking risks that could build members' trust in each other. These dysfunctions occur because of how the group is led, characteristics of the members, and the expectations of and support from the environment in which the group operates.

You may have people in your group whose behaviors are difficult. For instance, their behavior is argumentative, loud, stubborn, insensitive, or demanding attention. There may be others who are reticent and need to be drawn out. And there may be pairs or triumvirates who disrupt the group by talking among themselves, forming coalitions to block actions and prevent decisions, or forming cliques that exclude others.

To overcome these weaknesses and deal with problem behaviors, groups need to spend time together, get to know one another, communicate, plan, assess, and strategize. Control mechanisms and structured group processes can help deal with disruptive members, such as clear agendas and round-robin discussions that give everyone a chance to speak. Generally if group members feel comfortable enough to trust one another's criticism while maintaining cohesiveness of purpose, they will get to the bottom of issues and solve problems. Strong groups have members who engage in conflict to resolve issues, reach consensus, commit to decisions and plans of actions, believe in accountability for carrying out the plans, and focus on the achievement of group results. You may need to consult a group facilitator to deal with difficult members, conflicts, and negotiations.

Goals and Feedback

Goals affect performance strategies and outcomes. Feedback on the effectiveness of these strategies influences future goals. This has been demonstrated by considerable research on individual behavior and productivity (Aube & Rousseau, 2005). Just as goals and feedback are important to individual performance, they are also important for group learning and task performance (see Appendix C). Strong goal commitment leads to successful, effective groups. Group leaders encourage goal commitment by creating explicit goals and clear incentives for individual and group performance.

Goals and feedback at the individual level combine with group-level goals and feedback to affect both individual and group-level outcomes. However, the goals and feedback you provide should depend on the nature of the task. If the task requires that members work interdependently, then goals and feedback should be at the group level. If the task requires that members work independently and then combine their individual units of performance, the goals and feedback should be at the individual level. Individual and group characteristics, such as the desire to acquire and apply new knowledge and attain the consequences of reaching performance objectives, affect how feedback is processed and the goals that are set.

Group Goals and Feedback Improve Group Performance; Individual Goals and Feedback Improve Individual Performance

How the processes of individual- and group-level goals and feedback affect individual and group performance were investigated in a study of seventy-nine three-person groups of undergraduate college students (DeShon, Kozlowski, Schmidt, Milner, & Wiechmann, 2004). The students engaged in a task that seated the group members in front of simulated radar consoles where contacts with different priorities and patterns of movement appeared. Group members could communicate with one another as they contacted each other on the radar screen, collected information, and made decisions about whether to take action. Each group member was responsible for one of three sectors on the display but could also monitor and work on their fellow group members' displays. After each event, the group members received feedback about how they did as individuals and how the group performed as a whole by determining total points for that event.

Individuals set performance goals for themselves and for their group prior to each event. The results showed that higher goals led to better performance at the individual and group levels. Moreover, group members who received only individual feedback focused their attention and effort on individual performance, and this resulted in the highest levels of individual performance. Group members who received only group-level feedback tended to focus on group performance, and this resulted in the highest group-oriented performance. Members who received both individual- and group-level feedback were unable to optimally capitalize on the feedback. Apparently receiving a single, focused source of feedback (individual or group) resulted in better individual or group performance than receiving feedback at the individual and group level simultaneously.

Feedback depends on the nature of the group task and what is important to emphasize: group or individual performance. If the task requires that members work interdependently and group performance is a priority, then the goals and feedback should be at the group level. Conversely, if the task requires that members work independently, then goals and feedback should be individual. Combining group and individual feedback together can lead to confusion. However, even when group-level performance is critical and the primary focus, individual-level feedback that helps members understand how they contribute to the group's performance may be valuable. For instance, this may be feedback to individuals about how well they work with others or how they can improve their coordination. (We say more about giving and receiving feedback in Appendix C.)

Continuous Quality Improvement Groups

Group processes aimed at quality improvement are called Continuous Quality Improvement (CQI) or sometimes Total Quality Management (TQM). These groups follow standardized guidelines for group process. The group leader and a professional group facilitator guide the group through a predetermined process that is the same for all CQI groups. A typical process uses the following steps:

1. Define the problem.

   What happens in the activities? Use a flowchart to diagram the elements in the work process indicating what leads to what and what happens first, second, and so forth.

   What are the big problems? Use brainstorming or checklists to identify problems that are occurring. Look at the percentage of times each problem arises. This is called Pareto analysis. Separating the vital few from the trivial many, Pareto analysis determines the percentage of different types of problems and their source, often finding that the 80–20 principle applies: 80 percent of the complaints come from 20 percent of the customers.

   What are the causes of the most major problem? Use brainstorming to generate possible causes, and then analyze the root of each cause. In other words, work backward to develop a diagram that shows what causes what.

   Find and examine existing data about the frequency of each of the causes.

2. Starting with what is happening now, suggest changes that may help eliminate causes and ultimately alleviate the problem.

3. Test the changes; observe the effects.

4. Take permanent action; ensure that the solution is embedded in the new process.

5. Continue to monitor and make adjustments to maintain the gains.

   Note that different methods are used throughout this quality improvement process: brainstorming, checklists, Pareto analysis, and frequency charts, as well as feedback cycles that allow for adjustments and change over time. The members learn these techniques and are able to apply them again when they participate in other structured quality improvement group efforts. Quality improvement programs have been particularly successful in hospitals, since they are often mandated by accrediting bodies.

Getting Help

Leading a committee or task force does not have to be a do-it-your-self experience, especially if you have never done this before. In Chapter Four, we noted that group leaders should understand the value of facilitation and coaching. Large businesses may have professionals in an organization development department or the human resource department who can help. Alternatively, facilitators from outside the firm can be hired. These may be independent consultants or members of firms that specialize in organizational change. (For information about certification for professional facilitators and finding a competent facilitator, see the Web site of the International Association of Facilitators: http://www.iaf-world.org.) Here are some suggestions for finding help to facilitate your group.

Identify One or More People Who Can Help Facilitate

A facilitator provides guidance, serves as a sounding board, helps plan meetings, and attends the meetings as an observer and advisor. In particular, the facilitator can handle the following tasks:

- Run icebreakers at the start of the group.
- Educate the group on process methods such as brainstorming.
- Record interaction process analyses, and provide the results back to the group. (See Bales's method for interaction process analysis later in this chapter.)
- Lead a discussion about group process at the end of each meeting. Ask the group to reflect on how well the group is doing.

- Stop a meeting that is dysfunctional (perhaps everyone is talking at once), and ask the group to step back, observe what is happening, and refocus.

- Help the leader select and evaluate members, plan ahead, prepare agendas, offer ways to control difficult members (those who talk too much or go off on tangents), and suggest assignments.

At meetings, the facilitator can observe and lead a process discussion, asking the group to step back from their task and reflect on their conversations and how they are working together. The facilitator can collect some data on the frequency with which each member contributes, showing the members the unevenness in their discussion and tactfully giving more vocal members the idea that they should let others speak.

A professional facilitator or organization development expert can add considerable value, especially if you bring the consultant in from the beginning. Waiting until the group is midway through the task before bringing in a consultant may challenge strongly held decisions that have already been made by group members and undermine the cohesiveness of a group that has already invested time and effort in the process. Group members may feel threatened because their efforts and assumptions are being challenged. Also, a consultant who is a member of the group from the start will share the group history and commitment to the group goal (Freedman, 2000).

Ask Another Group Member to Help Facilitate the Group

Sometimes one or more other group members can be a facilitator while also contributing to the group discussion. You can ask another member to take minutes, record ideas on a flip chart, or be a sounding board and source of advice for you after the meeting. But do not give the impression that you are playing favorites, giving one or more other members confidential information or allowing him or her to have more control than others. This leads to cliques and can disgruntle members quickly, especially those who do not see themselves as part of the clique.

If you want one or more other members to help you organize or facilitate the group, do not start by calling your friends on the committee between meetings to gripe about how things are going. Rather, ask one person to serve as facilitator. This will give the individual the freedom to redirect the group when the discussion goes off on a tangent or to signal you that it is time for a break.

Get Outside Advice and Coaching

Meet with an executive, mentor, or professional in the organization development field and describe what is going on in the group to get an objective view. Sometimes it helps just to talk over what is happening with someone who is not involved and does not have a vested interest in the group's work. You might invite the person to attend a group meeting and then give you feedback privately after the meeting.

Run a Training Session on Group Skills

If the group seems to be bogged down, unable to make decisions or always embroiled in conflict, you might suggest to members that you invite someone to run a training session for the group. You could arrange this without talking to the group first, but it will be accepted better if the group members agree beforehand that this would be worthwhile. After all, they will be devoting their time and energy to the session. Management consultants and trainers are available to do such work. If your committee is part of a nonprofit organization, you might look for a faculty member in the field of organizational behavior in the business school of a local university who would be willing to do the work pro bono or for a small fee. Although some conflict can be healthy, you may need some help if it becomes so confrontational that group interactions are stifled. Your group may need resources and skills to accomplish its goals.

Look outside the group for resources you cannot provide. In other words, know when to ask for help.

Find Resources to Help the Group Acquire New Knowledge and Skills

There are many books with exercises that can help group process. (You are reading one now, of course.) Your local bookstore or library will have resources on group development that you might want to consult.

Be a Role Model for Effective Member Behavior

As the group leader, remember that you are a role model for the other group members. Just like a parent, if you are respectful of other members, invite others to speak, and listen closely, chances are the other group members will follow suit. If you do most of the talking, give others' opinions short shrift, and argue, then this will become the tone for the meetings, and others will feel free to behave the same way.

In the case of the fundraising group mentioned in Chapter Five, the pastor became the facilitator for the leader. After the first committee meeting, the pastor met with the committee chair to talk about how the first meeting went. The pastor helped the chair write agendas for future meetings, made suggestions for how the leader could handle a recalcitrant member who seemed to disagree with everything, and offered ways for the group to generate and evaluate ideas in an orderly way using brainstorming and multivoting.

Keeping Members Motivated

Once the group is actively working on the task, members need to stay focused and motivated. Consider the following questions: How do you continue to have meaningful discussions with everyone participating? And how do you encourage the group to remain open to new ideas?

Diagnose the Stage of Group Development

What you do may depend on the stage of your group's development. As we said in Chapter Three, groups go through fairly predictable stages, which may repeat as the group reverts to an earlier stage to handle a problem, for instance, moving back from performing to storming. Table 6.1 offers some interventions that may enhance each stage of development.

Give Group Members a Chance to Experiment

One way to keep people stimulated and involved is to give them the chance to experiment with different ways of doing things.

Table 6.1 Interventions by Stage of Group Process

Stage	Intervention
Forming	Begin with introductions and icebreakers.
Storming	Use round robins for brainstorming and expressions of opinion to give everyone a chance to speak; use multivoting to select among alternative objectives.
Norming	Have clear agendas and take minutes; agree to a process of making motions and voting by majority rule; teach structured methods such as brainstorming, multivoting, flowcharting, or root cause analysis. The facilitator can offer a workshop on these techniques, or you can teach them to the group.
Performing	Follow structured methods and processes; stop for discussion about process—discussions about how well the group is working together and what they can do better. Try team-building exercises such as the icebreakers, or hold a retreat for devoting a concentrated period of time to the task away from daily activities (see Chapter Five).
Adjourning	Sponsor a thank-you event. Provide feedback to the group as a whole (you can do it, ask the facilitator to do it, or, better yet, both of you give feedback). Ask the group for feedback about your leadership and about the group process. Meet with members individually to give them individual feedback.

Example: Getting the Group Moving

A committee formed to find a new location for a community's food pantry serving the poor. The group had a month to get the job done. Following the town supervisor's recommendation for committee members, the chair of the committee, Sharon Crandall, invited the owner of a local restaurant and the head of a local accounting firm to join the group. They readily accepted, and both came early to the first meeting to talk to the committee chair. The restaurateur took Sharon aside and said that she would be very happy to donate left-over food to the pantry every day; however, she was concerned about the new location. She knew that there was a possible location two buildings down from her restaurant, and she was worried that this would be bad for business. The accountant also took Sharon aside and said that he knew little about the operations of a food pantry and that tax season was coming up, so he would not have much time to spend on the effort. Fortunately, there were several long-time residents of the community on the committee who had done volunteer work for the food pantry. One was in real estate and was knowledgeable about available locations.

The first meeting was taken up with introductions and a briefing from the food pantry director about why they needed to relocate and what the needs were. The pantry did not have to be in prime real estate. It needed enough space for storage, and it needed to be readily accessible for people to drop off donations and, of course, for the needy clients to pick up goods. Many clients walked to the facility from several large apartment complexes in town, so it had to be fairly centrally located.

Here's what Sharon said about the group discussion:

This was a strange committee. On the one hand, we all knew how important the food pantry was to needy people in our community. We felt good about the work of the pantry, and the town government was very supportive. But some members on the committee just didn't want the pantry in their backyards, so to speak. They were on the committee to be sure that the pantry remained an invisible initiative except to those who needed it. The owner of the restaurant was at first pretty shy about her viewpoint, letting me know but not saying much at the group meetings. But every time someone suggested a place that was near her restaurant, she was quick to point out why it wouldn't work. Meanwhile, the accountant kept looking at his watch. I don't know why he bothered to show up. I was concerned that this whole effort was not as simple as it seemed at first. It wasn't just a matter of finding a vacant store or building we could rent or buy. We needed to evaluate the space in relation to the pantry's needs. This included arranging for some site visits as well as collecting data about parking, town ordinances, space and electrical facilities for the pantry's two large refrigerators, dry storage, and security. Since time was of the essence, we decided at the first meeting that we would meet three times a week for the first two weeks. Some members of the committee seemed bored with these details and stopped coming to meetings. I wasn't sure I had the best people on the committee. I was afraid that they didn't know or care enough about the food pantry and they didn't have the time to spend. But I didn't think I had the time to find new members.

One way to focus group members' motivation and attention is to ask for their input, give them a visible assignment that they cannot easily slough off without others knowing that they didn't do their job, and give them a chance to try out new ideas. Brainstorming and thinking creatively helped here. Here is what happened according to the accountant on the committee:

I have to be frank. This wasn't my cup of tea. It's not that I didn't care about the food pantry. I just hadn't had anything to do with it before I got the call from Sharon. I was trying to build a business in the community, and I didn't want to say no, that I wasn't interested and didn't have time. So, okay, I went to the first meeting and listened without much interest. At the second meeting, I got fed up with some of the members saying that people wouldn't want to use the pantry if others could see them coming in. What they really meant is that they didn't want poor people around their businesses. I didn't attend the next two meetings, and Sharon called to ask why. I gave some excuse but agreed to come to the next meeting. This is when I got hooked. Sharon admitted that we weren't making much progress. Then someone, I'm not even sure who, suggested that we step back a bit to think about what we were trying to do. Sharon jumped on the idea.

We started by reviewing the minutes from the first meeting at which the director of the pantry listed what kind of space was needed. Sharon wrote down each requirement on a flip chart and then asked us to suppose what would happen if the requirement couldn't be met. What else could the pantry do? So, for instance, one requirement was a central location. Suppose the pantry had to be on the outskirts of town. One committee member said we could have a delivery service. Another suggested a ride service. Another idea was bus vouchers. Still another was having a remote storage facility and bringing orders to the town hall once a week. I wasn't sure any of these ideas would work, but this started something new. We began to think creatively. Someone else suggested that perhaps the current facility could be expanded. Someone else said that maybe we should have multiple smaller locations using available town space. Someone else suggested that we didn't need a permanent solution necessarily but could try different methods of operation. I volunteered to make some calls to local businesses to ask them about any free warehouse space they might have, at least on a temporary basis.

Opening a group to brainstorming can be a freeing experience. It can present members with ideas that they might not have thought of otherwise. One idea begets another. Everyone has a chance to participate, and people get the idea that it is okay to try new things. They do not have to wait to be told what to do or begged to participate; instead, they can take some ownership of the problem and show initiative to take on a task that they think needs to be done.

Deal with Problem Behaviors

Any group is likely to have individuals who do not cooperate or even create problems. Rather than think of these individuals as problem people, think of their behaviors as problems. There are no silver bullets or magic solutions to deal with these issues. You need patience and some insight into human behavior. A few suggestions for coping are set out in Table 6.2.

Table 6.2 Suggestions for Dealing with Difficult Behaviors

Individual focus: *Generally get to know members before the first meeting. Talk to each individually. Determine how they feel about being part of the group and the issues that are of concern to them.*

Argumentative statements	Ask others to speak; use a round-robin technique going around the room; focus on the argument (put it in writing on a flip chart and ask the group to generate reasons for and against, brainstorm resolutions, and call for a vote).
Continually disagreeing; nay-saying, being stubborn	Have a clear agenda. Give the person the chance to speak, then say, "We're not going to resolve this now, so let's move on." Having the agenda allows you to move to the next point.
	Ask for alternative positions, and jot them on a flip chart for all members to see; apply majority rules vote to resolve issues.

(Continued)

Table 6.2 Suggestions for Dealing with Difficult Behaviors, Continued

Talking loudly	Peer pressure may help. Let other group members ignore the member, suggest that this individual calm down, or give others a chance to speak.
Being interpersonally insensitive—talking over others, insulting others	Take the individual aside and point out what he or she said and how others seemed to react; suggest alternative behaviors the person can use in the future.
Getting attention	Interrupt ("Let's hear from someone else now."); call other members by name, and ask for their opinions.
Being reticent	Call on members who haven't said much; go round robin so everyone speaks; ask the people who do not usually speak to start discussions.
Speaking too long	Tell everyone they have a maximum of three minutes to talk, and have one member watch the clock and indicate when time is up.

Subgroup focus: *Before the first meeting, ask members who else they know in the group. Arrange place cards to seat people next to others they do not know. In future meetings, continue to use the place cards to mix up sitting arrangements.*

Talkers (pairs)	Ask for order and wait until everyone is quiet before continuing; speak to individuals in private about this behavior.
Coalitions that band together to disagree with a group initiative	Define the issue and enumerate pros and cons; then follow structured procedures for discussion and voting.
Cliques who exclude others	Mix seating; establish subcommittees that include people who do not usually work together.
A cabal (disgruntled members who meet outside the meeting and try to push their own agenda)	Don't try to fight it. Put it out in the open, and try to diffuse the issue. Acknowledge in a meeting of the larger group that you know some people have gotten together and want to move the group in another direction. Put the idea to the larger group before the others do. Ask that in the future, members express their opinions openly in the group rather than get together in the parking lot for private conversations before or after meetings.

Adjust to Different Communication Styles

Group leaders and members vary in their communication styles and skills. Leaders need to be sensitive to differing communication styles and be able to adjust to them and help the group adjust. Some people are interpersonally sensitive. They are able to perceive and understand emotions, regulate their own emotions, and evoke emotions in others. These skills are components of emotional intelligence (Mayer & Salovey, 1997; Riggio, Riggio, Salinas, & Cole, 2003). Other people are low in these skills. They fail to listen, do not respond appropriately to others, and seem only to express their own point of view repeatedly. Communications involve behaviors (eye contact, posture, gestures, voice, facial expression, use of space, use of notes and visual aids), statements of content (clarity, succinctness, impact, and memorability), and interaction (ability to engage the listener, handle difficult issues, ask others for their opinions, clarify, and overcome hostility). Table 6.3 provides some ways to handle people who vary in two dimensions of communication: assertiveness and responsiveness (for scales to measure assertiveness and responsiveness, see *Communication Styles*, 1999).

Foster Collective Efficacy

Collective efficacy is the extent to which group members believe that the group can be successful. At the individual level, if people believe they are capable of performing well (this is the concept of self-efficacy), they are likely to exert more effort, and this affects the degree to which they persevere in the face of adversity. This applies at the group level as well. In fact, there is a positive relationship between collective efficacy and later group performance such that believing the group will be successful is important to the group actually doing well.

How Collective Efficacy Affects Group Performance

The value of collective efficacy was demonstrated in a study of the performance of ten intercollegiate football teams at U.S. universities

Table 6.3   Responding to Different Communication Styles

Communication Styles	Responsiveness	
Assertiveness	High	Low
High	You know where they stand, and they accurately perceive what is going on. They are clear and are able to handle difficult situations directly, using a range of behavioral skills to listen, respond, and express their viewpoint.	They state their mind and ignore you and everyone else. You need to control their floor time, ask them to repeat what others say, or clarify the different perspectives. Writing alternatives on a flip chart so everyone sees the same thing may help. They do not care about engaging the listener.
Low	Generally they are perceptive in understanding the situation; however, you are not sure what their opinion is, so request their input and feedback.	They are not engaged. You need to test whether they are listening (for example, ask them to repeat others' perspectives) and request that they express their own opinion.

(Myers, Feltz, & Short, 2004). Surveys were collected from players twenty-four hours before their games. Team members were asked to rate their confidence in their team's ability to outplay the opposing team on a variety of measures and ultimately win the game. They were also asked to rate their individual self-efficacy on such items as their confidence in their ability to outperform their opponent, ability to bounce back from performing poorly, perform their individual position successfully, and commit fewer penalties. Collective efficacy, the average of responses on these items across team members, was positively related to performance. That is, groups that were higher in collective efficacy before a game performed better. Also, performing poorly led to higher levels of collective efficacy for future games. This may be because games in which the teams did poorly were against tough competition. Also, coaches may have spent more time working with the team during the week prior to the next game, thereby boosting their confidence. Within weeks across teams, the prior week's performance was positively related to collective efficacy, suggesting a reciprocal relationship between efficacy and group performance (that collective efficacy increases performance and vice versa). Each individual member's self-efficacy was not related to team performance, indicating that team performance is very much a function of members' beliefs about how well the team as a whole will do, not on how they themselves will do.

Collective efficacy solidifies and influences group performance when the task requires that group members work together closely and depend on each other to accomplish the work. If group members are not interdependent, they have no basis for developing collective efficacy. Each member's self-efficacy becomes important to group performance under these circumstances (Katz-Navon & Erez, 2005).

Consider your group's collective efficacy. Ask members how likely they are to have a successful outcome, deliver their product on time, increase their sales, or whatever else the focus of the group happens to be. This should be an indicator of the extent to which individuals will exert effort and how well the group will actually do.

Organize Subgroups

A multigroup system is made up of two or more groups that work independently, sequentially or interdependently, toward hierarchical goals. Independently working groups are called pooled arrangements. An example is a group of people having a dinner party. One "group" brings main dishes, another drinks, and another desserts. Together, the efforts of many groups add up to accomplishing the higher goal of having a potluck dinner. An example of a sequential arrangement is a group of bakers making batter, baking batter, and then frosting the cakes to sell at a bakery. Many have to be baked to reach the store's goals. However, they cannot bake the cake until the batter is ready or frost the cake until it is baked. An example of an intensive or interdependent arrangement is an automobile assembly line. The car keeps moving on the line, and three or four people might be adding different parts to each car as it moves along. Several cars move, and several different kinds of parts are placed by several groups at once while the line moves.

Preplanning is especially important in subgroups that work independently and then join together to complete a task or produce a product. Advanced coordination is less important in subgroups that are highly interdependent because they work together intensively as the task is carried out or a product is produced.

The Importance of Preplanning and Coordination Depends on Degree of Subgroup Interdependence

A study of simulated multiteam systems showed that subgroup coordination determined the importance of preplanning (Marks, Mathieu, DeChurch, Panzer, & Alonso, 2005). There were forty-six combat teams of four people, two of them computer team members with whom the live members interacted during the simulation. First, transition planning took place, in which live team members mapped out strategies for hitting targets and accomplishing the multiteam goals. Three scenarios were run. In one, the teams worked independently of each other in a pooling arrangement to reach the goals. In the second, the teams worked sequentially: the actions of some teams could not take place until other teams had taken action. In the third, teams worked simultaneously to hit targets and reach goals. The study found that there was less difference between the sequential and pooling arrangements than there was between the intensive arrangements and both the pooling and sequential. In addition, they found that the effects of transition planning on team outcomes depended on how independently members worked. Teams worked more independently in the pooled and sequential conditions. When they worked face-to-face (interdependently), planning was not as important because decisions were made on the fly. When teams worked in the pooling or sequential patterns, the planning was important for effective team performance. There was less on-the-job interaction, so preplanning was needed for players to understand expectations. This led to better outcomes at the multiteam level.

Tools to Facilitate Group Process

Three important tools in the group process are taking minutes (perhaps this is obvious, but it should never be taken for granted), interaction process analysis, and use of electronic communications technologies.

Taking Minutes

Assign someone in the group to take minutes, or ask the group to elect a secretary. Minutes are important records of process and accomplishment. They show who made commitments and, over time, whether these commitments were met. They also are a record of decisions. Reviewing minutes from the previous meeting at the start of each new meeting can avoid rehashing the same issues. Minutes also become the historical archive of the group and may be useful to future committees or task forces tackling similar projects.

Clear minutes offer the leader a quick, efficient way to review group process and outcomes. Knowing who completed assigned tasks on time will help the leader determine who deserves credit or perhaps material rewards, such as a one-time pay bonus. In addition, knowing who is not passing muster will help the leader decide how to rearrange the group, giving assignments to reliable members or consulting in the future with insightful members.

Taking minutes can be daunting. Record keepers have a tendency to write too much, recording every comment and who said it. For long, complex meetings with many participants, there is a danger that the minutes will be long and convoluted and the motions and actions taken will be buried in an overwhelming amount of text. Secretaries should be careful to limit the text to important discussion points that lead to motions, votes, and actions. The group leader should ask the secretary to read the motion before the vote to be sure it is recorded accurately and that everyone understands it.

Another way to record minutes is in outline or chart format with three columns: one for topics discussed, the second for other related points of discussion, and the third for decisions and actions. Exhibit 6.1 shows the minutes from a meeting of a two-person group, your authors. This chart method provides a quick view of what was voted on during the meeting and what actions will be taken by which group members between this meeting and the next.

The chart method for recording minutes clearly outlines decisions made and who will perform each action. The results of motions should be listed in the right-hand column along with who will perform the action voted on. Accountability is established because the group can easily review the minutes and see who is doing what. This is an objective way to review accountability. It also gives the group a clear idea of whether they are making decisions and carrying them out. Members can see if the same ideas are revisited meeting after meeting. Also, the minutes will show if the group is making progress toward the goal.

The meeting agenda is an important tool for taking minutes. Most agendas outline the topics that will be covered at the meeting. These topics can be the points in the left-hand column of the chart. The secretary can record them on the chart before the meeting begins, making it easier for the note taker to follow the discussion as it ensues. Another tool is a sign-in sheet that lists the group members' names. It should be passed around at the start of the meeting,

Exhibit 6.1 Sample Minutes in Outline Format

Authors' Meeting

Conference Room

January 15th, Noon to 1 P.M.

Topics Discussed	Discussion	Decisions and Actions
Chapter Six	• Discussion focused on who would finish the draft of the chapter and begin editing it. • Discussed problems with sending information and ideas between the two authors. • Considered how to create and store electronic files so both authors could access them.	The following decisions were made: • Manny will complete the chapter. • Marilyn will write annotations of the literature and edit the chapter. • All information will be e-mailed from author to author and clearly dated for reference. • Files will be stored on a "stick" kept in a common area both can access.
Case studies	• Discussed how many case studies to use and how much detail they would include.	The following motions were passed: • Marilyn will write the character descriptions, questions, and processes. • Manny will integrate the information into the text of the chapter. • Marilyn will revise and edit the chapter when it's done.

Attendees: Manny, Marilyn

Absent: No one

Next meeting: January 16th

and members should sign in and return the list to the minute taker so that the records accurately reflect who was present.

Consider tape-recording meetings. However, do not wait to review the entire tape before taking minutes. Take good notes during the meeting, and use the tape to refresh your memory if points are unclear or you don't recall something. Write the minutes as soon after the meeting as possible so that you remember as much as possible.

The secretary should consider using a notebook computer to take notes during the meeting, even filling in a blank chart on the computer. This will save considerable time later. However, the secretary needs to be a good typist. The hunt-and-peck method does not work in fast-paced meetings.

Interaction Process Analysis

More than a half-century ago, Robert F. Bales, a professor at Harvard College for many years, developed an interaction process analysis for examining patterns of small group interaction during problem-solving and decision-making. Bales (1950) divided group members' statements during meetings into (1) social and emotional exchanges, such as personal remarks, social conversation, self-disclosure, and expressions of concern or disapproval, and (2) task-oriented exchanges, such as asking for or giving information, opinions, examples, or advice. A given statement made by a group member can fall into one or more categories. Although the Bales Interaction Process Analysis was initially used as a research tool for carefully analyzing recorded group interactions, the method is also useful for assessing group process. An observer (for instance, the group facilitator if there is one, a guest, or one of the members) can be asked to watch the group interaction and, for each member, categorize each statement the individual makes. The observer puts a mark every time a statement fits into the category. Since making these ratings is a fairly intensive process, several observers may be needed, each tracking and categorizing the responses of three or four people.

Even without systematic observations, group leaders can give feedback to group members about their social, emotional, and task exchanges. This feedback may help redirect the group members, who may not realize how the way they interact with each other is affecting the group. Maybe they need to spend more time on task than in social conversation. Maybe they need to be reassuring and complimentary of each other. Perhaps they need to laugh more.

Electronic Group Support Systems

Technology can be useful to help a group in many ways. Of course, virtual groups rely on electronic communications. Groups that meet face to face are likely to rely on e-mail and other electronic means for communications in between meetings and as a method for recording and sharing information. Consider the following electronic tools:

- *Intranet Web site*: This can be a repository of minutes, reports, news articles, and data. It can be a means of sharing databases, allowing members to do their own analyses and share them for discussion since there may be different ways of looking at the same set of data. Members can download a data table, run analyses, and provide results. The software records data on the number of visits by individual members to track use. Group members can request or run their own reports from the online databases.

- *Chatroom*: Web sites can offer live chats at designated times. Alternatively, the site can provide a discussion board for members' comments. Members log in at times that are convenient for them and join the conversation by reading what others said and leaving a remark (a type of blog). The leader can pose questions and gather opinions and even call for a vote.

- *Online seminar* (sometimes called a webinar): An expert presents a slide show and audio discussion, with an opportunity for questions and answers from the group members, who may be together in one room listening to a remote presentation or at their individual computers in their offices or homes.

- *Podcast:* Presentations, discussions, and announcements can also be posted electronically and downloaded to iPods, cell phones, or computers for group members who cannot make meetings or to keep members informed, especially when they are geographically dispersed.

- *Teleconference:* Using telephones, perhaps combined with a Web camera or video, groups at different sites join in a meeting.

Setting up a Web site and database may require the consultation of an information technology specialist and access to a server. However, many people who are not information technology experts know how to do this. You can ensure security by limiting access to those with IDs and passwords. Also, various Web sites and Internet access providers offer users the chance to make their own Web pages and set up groups for discussion. Users need to guard against public access if this is a concern. It may not be, and in some situations, for instance, in government, you may want the public to have ready access to minutes and an opportunity to join a public discussion.

Making Progress

Making progress means getting work done. Some work may happen at meetings, but for the most part, meetings are when issues are reviewed, decisions are made, and further tasks are identified and assigned. As tasks are identified, people may volunteer to take them on, individually or in subgroups, or the committee chair or task force leader may ask members to be responsible for them. The chair then holds them accountable, setting deadlines and asking for a report or review of the work at the next meeting. Public accountability increases the chances that the work will be done and done well. Generally people want others to think highly of them, especially their peers—in this case, their fellow group members and their leader.

Making Decisions

Decisions must be made expeditiously, especially if there are deadlines. In carrying out any task, there are multiple decisions along the way. In the case of the fundraising committee in Chapter Five, the members needed to decide which people to honor, where and when the event should be held, and ways of issuing invitations and raising sponsorships, not to mention many details about the event itself. In the case of the building location committee in this chapter, decisions needed to be made about the nature of the space, accommodations that may be needed, key aspects of the space about which they were not willing to compromise, elements of the lease or purchase, and, ultimately, the decision to move ahead with a particular location.

Before a decision can be made, the alternatives need to be identified and evaluated. This might be done by a subcommittee of members who review the issues thoroughly before the meeting and present a report and recommendations for action. The group leader needs to guard against the group's rehashing the subcommittee's work. The other committee members may need to ask questions to clarify the recommendation, raise issues that the subcommittee did not think of, and express their opinions. Eventually the decision will be called for a vote, or the leader may make the decision after hearing all viewpoints. The leader may ask a member to make a motion and open the floor for discussion, perhaps for a designated period of time or until someone on the committee calls the question for a vote.

Delegating Work

Group leaders may be tempted to do all the work themselves. They need to resist that temptation. It may seem easier to just do the work, particularly if members do not know just what to do or will be asking the leader continuously for guidance. The leader may want things done in a certain way and may not trust members to do exactly what he or she has in mind. The leader may unwittingly want to be a martyr or may want to take credit for the work. Nevertheless, leaders need to be open to members' input. (Otherwise, why bother having a group?) Members need to be involved and take responsibility for the work, especially if they ultimately need to own the product, that is, feel that it is theirs, abide by whatever decisions are made, and implement them. Also, of course, members may have the skills, knowledge, and experience to do the work better than the leader could ever do alone. If either condition is true (members have valuable input or they need to act on the group's decisions, or both), the committee or task force chair should be sure that the group members know who is responsible for what.

Holding Members Accountable

Accountability is being held responsible for one's actions. Responsibility implies there is a consequence, that is, a reward for meeting obligations and a punishment (or absence of reward) for failing to meet them. Accountability works because people care about the outcome, and they want others to know they are reliable. There are four necessary ingredients for holding people accountable: (1) establishing clear expectations, (2) preparing people to meet those expectations with needed training and support, (3) monitoring performance, and (4) attaching consequences to the results (Baumeister, 1982).

Accountability is a way of saying that you mean business—that this is important work and that you as the group leader expect that members will meet their commitments. Otherwise they will not take you seriously, and work will not get done. Accountability enhances involvement and commitment. Assigning tasks and reviewing the results in public is a way to increase accountability. Requiring that members justify their actions further increases feelings of accountability.

Avoiding Dead Ends

When your group seems to have hit a dead end, that is, when progress seems to have halted and you keep going over the same old issues without making progress, here are some strategies to try:

Ask the group to think about how they would answer the questions, Where are we? What should we do next? Go around the table, and let people speak their minds. Give each person a time limit but free range to take the group anywhere they think it should go as long as they stick to the objectives. Summarize what is said on a flip chart. If people are reticent about suggesting new directions, ask them to write down what has been working and what has not in the group. Have a group member collect the ideas, without names on them, and summarize them at the next meeting.

If a change in objectives is possible, ask the group if you should change the objectives. If they say yes, pair them up for ten to fifteen minutes of discussion. Then ask the pairs to summarize their conclusions. What ideas did they have for new objectives or changing the way the group is working?

Have members pair up and explain to each other what new information each has found since the previous meeting. Ask them to decide which information is most important to present to the whole group. Then give them time to present it. This builds closer relationships between members and gives them time to absorb new information. It also allows them to get feedback at a lower level before the entire group is exposed to their ideas.

Create imaginary scenarios that might be something like your end results. Present the scenarios at your meeting, and ask members to pair up to discuss them. Any idea that changes the way your group thinks about the product might generate fresh thinking.

Determining What Needs Improvement

Think about your group process and how things are going. What issues do you need to work on most? We will return to this topic in Chapter Eight when we focus on evaluating group process and outcomes. Meanwhile, here are some items you can rate to help you examine your group's process.

Rate the importance of each of the following for a group you are leading using a scale from 0 = no importance to 5 = major importance.

_____   Keeping people motivated

_____   Keeping people on task

_____   Involving everyone

_____   Motivating and involving from the start

_____   Getting help

_____   Maintaining motivation

_____   Dealing with interpersonal problems

_____   Making decisions

_____   Preparing for the next meeting

_____   Reflecting on the group process and outcomes; identifying lessons learned

Summary

This chapter examined ways to improve teamwork. Goals and feedback are essential ingredients for making progress. We described structured processes that quality improvement teams use as methods you might want to borrow. As you proceed, you may need help from a facilitator or coach; never hesitate to get some help. We considered ways to maintain members' motivation and develop a sense of collective efficacy in the group. The chapter described some tools for facilitating group process, such as taking good minutes and ways to analyze the interaction among your group members. Think about how to assess group progress all along the way. Then be deliberate about bringing your group to a successful conclusion, including giving members feedback and thanking them. We leave you with the following recommendations for improving teamwork:

- Set goals and give feedback. Groups in which members work independently and then combine outputs need individual goals and feedback; groups in which members work interdependently, integrating their work as they progress, need group goals and group-level feedback.

- Consider the applicability of a step-by-step structure. This is the case with Continuous Quality Improvement/Total Quality Management groups. Members represent diverse functions and organization levels and need to work together. These groups use flowcharts to analyze work flows, identify problems or barriers, determine root causes, brainstorm improvement strategies, design and implement changes, evaluate outcomes, maintain these steps to hold the gains, and make adjustments as needed.

- Never hesitate to request help. Professionals, supervisors, and group members can provide valuable advice and ideas for improving group process.

- Foster collective efficacy. Groups do better when members believe the group can succeed.

- Use electronic communication methods.

- Plan in advance for how to integrate input from different members when the members will be working independently and then come together to meld their inputs, as a group would in producing a potluck dinner (in other words, reduce the potluck so you do not end up with all desserts). These are the groups that especially need individual goals and feedback.

- Make progress by delegating work, tracking and assessing deadlines met and tasks accomplished, and holding members accountable.

Chapter 7

HELPING YOUR GROUP LEARN TO GET BETTER

In this chapter, we show you how to help your group learn. Although your group may be short term, members need to learn how to work effectively with each other. Indeed, a short-term group needs to learn quickly. Generally, small groups have some time to improve the way members work together. Think of your group as a living system that is continuously evolving. Even short-term groups evolve. What happens during the first meeting (for instance, how well the group members get to know one another) will influence what happens later. Groups learn as the members learn how to work with each other. They learn to establish effective routines for interacting, and they can improve how they work together over time. Even groups that have a very short duration are learning opportunities, and what you find from participating in a group, as a leader or member, will help you the next time you join a group.

This chapter examines how to recognize and do something about external pressures you may face. We suggest ways to increase group members' readiness to learn, for example, by helping them be more open to new ideas and sensitive to other group members' thoughts and feelings. You will learn how to help group members adapt to outside pressures, share and apply new knowledge and skills, and, if necessary, make a major shift in what you do and how.

After reading this chapter, you will be able to:

- Diagnose pressures from within your group and outside that push the group to do its best.

- Determine directions for improvement—for instance, whether your group needs to adapt, learn needed skills and knowledge, or invent different ways of working together depending on pressures from within and outside the group.

- Determine whether your group members are ready to collaborate— to share information and make decisions together.

- Foster a learning environment, even in short-term groups, so the group members do their best.

Group Learning

What does it mean for a group to learn, and is learning important in a short-term group? Does a short-term group have time to improve its performance? How does it do this? Are clubs, boards, and other ongoing groups that meet periodically able to learn over time, even when members and agendas change?

The answer to these questions is yes. Groups do learn, and they can quickly learn ways to improve their performance. Think of a group as a living system. A living system is dynamic, that is, constantly changing—sometimes rapidly, sometimes slowly. Think about your own group and what you do during meetings. You will probably realize that no two meetings are alike. Still, as the leader, you help your group find ways to work together as effectively as possible and to improve their performance: to make the most of every meeting, set goals, stick to deadlines, and (you hope) not get bogged down in arguments or internal politics.

As a system, a group receives input from the outside (for instance, from supervisors or other groups) and from within (that is, from you and the other members). It then uses this to produce a product and gets feedback about that product. As such, it reacts to and produces stimuli that cause it to change.

As a group process unfolds, members may learn how to act collaboratively. Individual members acquire knowledge and skills, and they convey these to other group members. In addition, members learn interaction patterns that take advantage of synergies that result from bringing together the expertise of the group members (Argote, 1999; Zaccaro, Hildebrand, & Shuffler, in press). Habits of interaction are established quickly in a group, setting the stage for bringing about later success, dealing with uncertainties and problems, and possibly facing failure. Group leaders and members facilitate the group process, for instance, by making recommendations and supplying useful resources, that help the group learn how to operate more effectively. Group leaders encourage and reward discovery, constructive controversy, and reflection. They act as a learning partner as they give feedback and coach individual members and the group as a whole (Zaccaro et al., in press). Group learning is really a function of group members' learning about themselves and each other as they interact.

In this chapter, we describe three patterns that groups can learn to help make themselves be more effective (Sessa & London, 2006):

1. They can learn how to adapt to pressures and change in the environment. This is *adaptive learning,* that is, learning how to adapt and then adapting when needed. For instance, a group might adapt to minor changes in the environment, such as a reduction in resources or a slightly different goal.

2. They can learn how to be proactive to find new resources (money, technology, information, ideas) and experiment by applying these resources in new ways to do their work. This is *generative learning,* that is, learning how to generate and try out new ways of interacting and thinking about an issue, the outcomes of which cannot be anticipated. The members may learn on their own (for instance, acquire knowledge about a new technology), share information, and suggest innovative ways for implementation. They take responsibility for generating knowledge and educating others (Raelin, 2006).

3. They can learn how to redirect their purpose and goals and transform themselves into new organizational structures to address changing needs. This is *transformative learning,* that is, learning how to create new visions and totally morph into a new group, perhaps for a very different purpose. The

committee chair, task force leader, or a member may have a totally new idea (for instance, a volunteer organization that decides to start a for-profit enterprise). The leader or member communicates a vision of this idea, champions the vision and convinces other group members that this is a great idea, and restructures the group to implement it.

Three factors can influence the extent to which a group learns to be adaptive, generative, or transformative, or a combination of these: (1) triggers or pressures for change in the environment, (2) members' readiness to learn (for instance, the extent to which they are open to new ideas), and (3) feedback. Group leaders and members can increase learning by emphasizing external pressures to which the group needs to respond, showing how to be open to new ideas and in other ways be ready to learn, and giving positive and negative feedback to direct or redirect the group.

Groups that are not adaptive, generative, or transformative may form habits that get stuck and can be dysfunctional. They are unlikely to adapt if the members feel no pressure to do so and are not ready to learn. If they feel pressure but are not ready, they may be forced to adapt, but they may not be generative in learning on their own, and they certainly will not see ways to transform themselves. Generative and transformative group learning requires an openness to new ideas, a willingness to experiment, and feedback about what works and what does not.

In this chapter, we describe and give examples of each type of learning, show how to influence it, and provide a set of questions that will help you diagnose how much your group has learned and whether it is prepared to adapt, be generative, or transform itself if need be, perhaps continuing its work in new and different ways.

Diagnosing How Your Group Learns

We begin with questions that help you understand whether your group is learning or is ready to learn in different ways:

What is happening in the group? Have members established ways to work with each other that seem to be effective? If not, perhaps they have learned dysfunctional patterns of behavior. There may be a combination of functional and dysfunctional behaviors. For instance, some members may seem to be uncooperative. Maybe the group has learned to tolerate these members or work around them. This might be okay for awhile, but how does the group handle an unexpected change, maybe an emergency? Do these disagreeable members get in the way?

What are the forces for learning and change? Are there demands on the group, perhaps sudden and unexpected ones, that necessitate that the group change what it is doing in some way? Are there forces from outside the group, perhaps an executive changing what she wants the group to do? Are there forces from within the group, perhaps the committee chair asking group members to put their differences aside and focus on a common goal? Maybe members of the group are introducing the need to change by bringing in new information, ideas, or suggestions.

To what extent is the group sensitive to pressures for change? Is the chair, or are the members, attuned to what others are saying about the group or others' expectations for the group? Do they monitor the environment? Or do they ignore it? How sensitive are they to pressures from within—for instance, to members who want the group to consider new information?

Are individual members and the group as a whole open to new ideas, sensitive to each other and to what is happening outside the group? Have they been working together long enough to demonstrate maturity, for instance, to know who is good at doing what, volunteer when something needs to get done and then follow through, act without being told what to do? If so, perhaps they are poised to learn and try new things?

Is there pressure for change, and are group members ready for change? If so, the group might be ready for generative learning and possibly transformative learning. Is there pressure for change, but members really want things to stay the same? In this case, the group might adapt but change as little as possible. Are group members open to new ideas and experimenting but there is little pressure to do things differently? In other words, why fix what isn't broke? Does the group as a whole feel that way but one or more members (or maybe the group leader) have a bright idea they are pushing?

What factors are barriers to learning and change? Do members resist change? Do they prefer the status quo even though conditions have changed? Why? Perhaps there are some influential members who value and guard their status or position in the group, even if it puts the group's survival at risk?

What factors facilitate learning? Do you as the group leader clarify pressures the group is under? Do members bring new ideas to the group? Are you open to trying new things—for example, throwing out the planned agenda and focusing on the new information or ideas?

You want your group to be able to adapt when needed. You also want it to be generative, to be open to new ideas and willing to try new things. You may want it to be ready and able to transform; however, this is probably a rarer occurrence and less necessary. Still, you may want to know, or at least think about, how to bring about transformation if conditions change radically (for instance, suddenly you are out of money). We next look at each type of learning and some examples. We tackle adaptive and generative learning first, then consider transformative learning.

Adaptive and Generative Learning

Adaptive learning means making minor alterations in the way the group operates. Groups that adapt learn how to be adaptive. In short, they learn how to be flexible and change their behavior when the need arises.

Generative learning is taking an idea and running with it. For example, one or more members have some knowledge or insight that they explain to the group. They educate the other members, and together they create ways to apply it. They implement the idea and fine-tune it as needed. They had no idea where this would lead when they started, but they were open to change and experimentation. In the process, they learn how to be generative, and they can do so in different ways in the future.

Example: Adaptive and Generative Learning

The sales manager in a printing company developed a partnership with an Internet Web page design firm. The sales manager, Jennifer Kline, and the head of print design, Mark Garcia, were assigned by the printing company's owner to work with their counterparts in the Internet company, specifically, the head of sales, Dave Jenkins, and the chief Web designer, Emily Caplowski. They would be responsible jointly for managing clients' jobs that required both print and Web media. At this early point in the partnership, everyone wanted to see how well things would work out. Jennifer, the printing sales manager, realized that this would change a lot of things and would require adapting to a new process. For instance, it would require tight coordination between the partners to be sure they were in sync in working on a client's projects. Otherwise, the Web and print design and content might be uncoordinated with different looks and time lines.

This new team started with a meeting to consider how they would work together. They decided to simulate a client project and then outlined the steps they would follow in some detail, using several examples from recent client projects to see how it would work. They created a new order form that detailed print and Web specifications together, set up weekly joint project meetings to review work in progress, and identified goals for how quickly they would turn around designs for presentation to a client.

The first client came down the pike several weeks later. Jennifer had a long-time print customer who wanted to start an Internet sales operation to go with its new print catalogue. Jennifer got the joint project team together to work on a proposal. They used the new

---

order form to indicate specs for the project, agreed to a time line so that print and Web media would be developed simultaneously, and worked out a suggestion for a design they felt would work in both print and the Web.

The client meeting was a disaster. It quickly became apparent to the joint project team that they had made some assumptions about how things would work that did not fit this first client. The client did not want the print and Web versions to look the same. They wanted each version to have contact information about the other (for instance, how to order a mail catalogue on the Web for any customer who might want to do so, and how to access the Web for customers who received the print catalogue). They wanted the Web version to be online as soon as possible, at least in a skeletal version that could be fleshed out over time. They wanted a young, hip look for the Web and a traditional, rich look for print, assuming that older customers would prefer the catalogue they were used to and younger customers would find them on the Web or go to the Web from the catalogue. The team needed to adapt quickly, The Web designers needed to move ahead fast while they stayed in contact with the print designers. The two looks offered the same product line, so they needed to think of ways to make the photographs work in both print and the Web.

The weekly meetings went out the window. Continuous communication was needed. The project team developed their own intranet process using a customized Web site that would allow them to have ongoing discussions and show each other their layouts. As this got going, they gave the client access to the intranet site about their project, so the client became integral to their vendor's partnership team. The team hoped that the intranet communication process would work for other clients, but this remained to be seen. They were beginning to realize that each client project would have its own idiosyncrasies.

What did the group learn?

- It was hard to foresee what interaction patterns would work best.
- Planning work processes helped the group members get to know each other.
- They were able to change their planned work processes quickly.
- They were able to adapt and be innovative with a new work process (the project intranet).
- They need to be ready to adapt and experiment with new ways of working in the future.
- They will discover ways of working together that they can adapt to fit new situations.
- Digital technology is changing both Web and print continuously, and they better be prepared to learn and experiment continuously. This will be a bumpy ride.

This group saw the pressure to learn and adapt from the client. Failure to adapt meant losing the business. If they had argued that the client had the wrong approach and that the right approach was what they had worked out in their initial planning meetings, they might have been headed for disaster. This is learning the hard way. Or they may have learned nothing at all since they would not have had a chance to change their behavior. They might have lost the client and blamed it on the client, not on their own intransigence. Chances are that this would have been a recipe for failure, and the partnership would have dissolved before it began.

As we noted in Chapter Five, groups develop a collective memory, which is knowledge of group members' expertise. This happens especially when the task requires different expertise and the members have this expertise and make each other aware of it when the group gets started. Groups that develop a collective memory system are able to apply it when they have to engage in other tasks that are similar and require the same range of expertise. Having this knowledge of each member's expertise helps the group learn individually and collectively. They learn about each other, draw on this knowledge when they confront a new task, and develop a deeper understanding of how to work together effectively. During initial stages of the task, members begin to associate individual members with specific areas of expertise. When they have new tasks, they need to notice the similarities and the basic principles about how to do the work that transfer to the new task. If they had a solid idea of each other's expertise at the start and this helped them during the first task, they are likely to develop more abstract, generalized knowledge of underlying principles of effective group interaction when they engage in the next task. For instance, they may learn that writing down assignments and taking detailed minutes is the best way to track members' commitments. They may learn later that the minutes can be made clearer by separating opinions by action items.

If there is some kind of disruption in the group or the task—for instance, the person who was taking minutes leaves the group—then the collective memory is lost unless it can be transferred or conveyed to someone else. Also, if the group is given a new task or the task they were working on changes, collective memory might actually hurt performance because it will no longer work. Any principles about how the group members should work together will not hold up and will quickly dissipate. In fact, the group might have been better off if it had not developed a strong idea of who has what expertise (Lewis, Lange, & Gillis, 2005).

When group members participate in generative learning, they work together effectively and promote further generative learning. This creates a collective memory about how to be generative, which makes future generative learning easier and more likely. The key to meaningful generative learning is continued communication, sharing of information and ideas, and experimentation with new ways to implement these ideas.

As we saw in the example of the alliance between a traditional printing firm and an electronic media firm, fixed ideas about how to work together, established without much experience, proved to be faulty. The group needed to go beyond these fixed ideas about roles and responsibilities and create new structures. A collective memory will evolve as they work together. They will acquire new expertise, share that expertise, and come up with new ideas about how things work in their business. Of course, this will be a continuous process, and the alliance may have to transform itself more than once. Collective memory is not set in stone; it is a dynamic, constantly evolving process that helps members know how to work together. Transformation is an exciting, engaging process.

Consider another example of how disruptions can usurp collective memory. A firm is sold, and the new owners install a new management team. A few people from the old company may be left, but the interrelationships with the new members of the firm are yet to be formed. Here, transformation is likely to be an anxiety-ridden, stressful process for the old timers, and perhaps a challenging, if not frustrating, process for everyone concerned, including the newcomers. The key to success here may be a leader who can communicate a vision of the new organization and get people to own it. This leads us to our next topic: transformative learning.

Transformative Learning

Transformation is the process of being a champion for an idea, communicating it to others in the group, and convincing the group to do something that is very different from what they have done before. A group can learn to be transformative by being open to new ideas, listening and discussing them, shaping the ideas in new directions, and then making major changes (such as finding new members, acquiring new knowledge, and changing work processes) to implement the ideas and take the group in new directions. The transformational leader may be the committee or task force chair, another member of the group, who then is supported by the chair, or an outsider who brings new ideas to the group.

Example: Transformative Learning

A union negotiation team unexpectedly became transformative learners. The leader of the group, Frank Jacobson, was an employee in a large food distribution company that sells to grocery stores. Frank was elected by the members of the union local to serve on the union's team to negotiate a new contract with management. He had considerable experience working on negotiation teams, but this was the first time he had led a team and was worried. He knew how important this was to his fellow workers and that they would blame him for years if the contract did not meet their expectations. He needed to show them he was strong, but he also had to work out a fair contract. If the union team would not budge on any demand, they would reach an impasse; the union would be forced to strike or they would be subject to mediation (or both). Was the membership willing to face the hardship of a strike? What issues were most important to them? Management wanted to reduce their costs and asked for givebacks. For instance, they wanted the members to contribute some of their own money to the pension plan each year and pay for a portion of their benefits.

Frank met with his fellow members on the negotiating team to determine their demands and work out a strategy. They would present their most important demands first and make it clear that this is what they wanted. They would then offer some concessions on less important issues. They would present a complete and fair plan and hope that management would agree that it was reasonable.

At the first negotiation meeting with management, each side presented its proposals. The flaw in the union's plan was quickly apparent: their most important demands were also management's key concerns, and management was not flexible, at least not at this early stage. This was not an unusual situation in labor negotiations, but somehow it was a surprise to the union team. Frank had wanted to rise above petty squabbles and show that he was a true visionary leader—someone the rank and file would follow and management would respect. This was clearly wishful thinking on his part.

From previous experience and from observing other labor negotiations, Frank knew several strategies to follow. He could go before the public and explain the union's position and hope for community support. He could stick to his guns and not budge. He could give in on some demands, but this would weaken the union's position. However, he had an idea: ever the optimist, he thought that maybe the negotiations would make more progress if the teams split—half of the union negotiators working with half of the management team on one set of issues and the other half working on another set. Neither of the union nor management subgroups would make commitments, only lay out a range of alternatives. Then the two groups would come together to share their results. The union and management teams would then separate for closer examination of their positions and determination of degree of flexibility around the different issues and ways of combining them (giving up a bit on one issue, gaining on another). They would then start the process again. The advantage, the union leader argued, is that they would be taking the time to examine the issues thoroughly, come up with ranges of alternatives, and review them together and separately before returning to the subgroups. The subgroups would really be a prenegotiation that prepared the teams for full-scale discussion when the full teams came together.

Frank prepared to present this idea to a joint meeting of the negotiation teams. It was a risk: his union members might think he was taking management's side, and management might think he had something up his sleeve. However, he knew the managers on the negotiating team, and he thought they trusted him. After all, they had worked together every day for years. Let them refine his suggestion or suggest another process. So he gave it a try, and it worked. They agreed to his suggested process, at least for one round of discussions. After the first meetings of the subteams, the joint teams came together to review the outcomes as planned. Dealing with a range of alternatives expanded each side's perspective and gave them more to work with. After several rounds, they reached an overall agreement. This could have backfired, with the union and management losing the trust in, and respect for, the union leader. As it was, the leader learned that it is okay to think broadly and not to assume something will not work before it is mentioned. The union negotiation team learned that it is okay for union members to be progressive and take a leadership role in shaping negotiation processes. This is not the sole prerogative of management or professional mediators. The management team learned that the union could be constructive in thinking about ways they could work together as well as possible outcomes. Maybe this spirit could transcend the negotiation table and apply to their daily work.

Perhaps this was a fluke. Labor negotiations do not always go so smoothly. Yet transformative leadership and learning is possible, even in labor negotiations. The union team leader's feeling at the start was excitement and anxiety. He wanted to become a respected leader and to do things differently. He did not want to be the old-school, cigar-chomping union official who refused to budge, no matter what the consequences to management or the rank and file. He recognized that times have changed. The union had benefited him and his coworkers. As the negotiations began, he worried about whether he had taken the best path. Management seemed to have the public on its side. A strike would cut off supplies to grocery stores in the area. He did not want to repeat what had happened in California when the United Food and Commercial Workers Union went on strike against Southern California supermarkets in October 2003. That strike lasted five months and involved 59,000 workers in more than 852 grocery stores. The issue was health care and benefits, as it was here. But the current situation was far less visible. Also, the California settlement was a model for what might be done here. Frank wanted his union and management to learn from California. Also, he wanted to get all the issues out on the table: pay, pension, and health care benefits. Providing maternity leave was another key demand. At the end of the negotiations, Frank had the following thoughts:

> I took a risk, and it paid off. I transformed the way our union thinks about negotiations, and management too. I suggested a new process for discussion. I think we all had a common goal to get this thing over with quickly. Maybe that's why it worked. Any other method might have been just as good. Who knows? I learned that I can be effective not only in making arguments but also by developing a process for discussion. The process is just as important as, and maybe more important than, our strategies and decisions. That's the take-home message for me.

In the next example, the curriculum development group in a local school system showed both generative and transformative group learning.

Example: Generative and Transformative Learning

The district superintendent had appointed a committee to discuss and make recommendations about the feasibility of an inclusion program that would take mentally disabled students out of resource rooms and place them in regular classrooms. This is not an unusual initiative; many schools have adopted the approach. Yet there was considerable disagreement within the district among teachers and parents about whether this was a good idea. The committee chair, Rosemary Akers, was an elementary school teacher. The committee consisted of several other teachers from the elementary, middle, and high schools and representatives of parents appointed by the parent-teacher organization in consultation with the school board. This was a large committee: eighteen in all—nine parents and nine teachers. Rosemary scheduled weekly meetings that continued for the first half of the school year. Parents and teachers paired up to research the issues within the different age groups and present their findings. The literature on inclusion and the experiences in other school districts was not in agreement. Clearly there was no one right way to approach this. If they were to try inclusion, teachers would need training and resources to make it work.

A teacher and parent who had been talking on the side before a meeting suggested giving inclusion a try. The committee could establish two field trials: one in the elementary school and one in the high school. Two groups of mentally impaired children would be selected in each school: one group to stay in the resource room and the other to be in the inclusion classroom. Each group would have a cross-section of mental disabilities, so the experimental and field groups would be similar. Teachers in the inclusion classrooms would receive training and have an adviser available to help with any problems that arose. The trial would last throughout the second half of the school year. The group also established measures to assess the outcomes: attitudinal measures of teachers and parents of the children and test scores on standardized tests of math and verbal skills appropriate for students in this group and independently scored evaluations of projects.

Essentially the group transformed itself from a committee that hashed through the issues and made recommendations to a field experiment task force. Members participated in designing the training, shaping the assignments, and developing measures. The group stayed together to oversee the experiment, analyze the results, and present a report to the superintendent and school board. Parents learned about pedagogy; teachers and parents learned about assessment methods; and they all learned to express their disagreement and create methods to examine the issues objectively, in this case using a range of measures.

The results after the first trial were that inclusion seemed to work for some students and not for others. The group, with the support of the superintendent and board, decided to continue their field trials the following year to understand student characteristics and classroom strategies that seemed to make a difference. They would implement a mixed strategy that included both inclusion and resource room pedagogy and apply assessment methods to evaluate what they were doing.

The committee effort continued for two more years, at which point the superintendent established an office of assessment and reassigned two teachers from the committee to work in the office, which became the responsibility of the system's assistant superintendent for curriculum development. In this way, the superintendent institutionalized the committee's transformative learning. The teachers and parents who were part of the committee and experiment, as well as others who observed the process, learned a great deal about experimental and field methods that they could apply to other curriculum issues.

Triggers and Readiness for Group Learning

These examples of generative and transformative group learning showed that the groups felt pressure for change and were ready for change; at least, they were open to new ideas and experimentation and therefore ripe for learning. They wanted to absorb new information and try new ways of working together. Perhaps the overriding concern in each case was that the members wanted their groups to succeed. Even in the labor negotiations, the members of the opposing group hoped for a reasonable resolution without rancor or high cost. If members of any of these groups had resisted change, the generative and transformative patterns of behavior and change would not have emerged.

Can groups be forced to learn? Probably not. Indeed no one can be forced to learn. They can be pressured and supported. However, living systems, whether they are individuals, groups, or organizations, will not learn unless they see the need and are willing to change their behavior. So what can you as a group leader do to stimulate and support your group's learning? You can focus on three types of initiatives:

1. Create learning triggers (pressures for change).

2. Increase readiness to learn.

3. Support the ways people learn (adaptive, generative, and transformative learning).

Table 7.1 presents some ideas to facilitate triggers, readiness, and learning.

To examine your group's tendency to apply adaptive, generative, or transformative learning, you need to know something about the pressures the group is under, the group's readiness for learning, and how the members have reacted to pressures for change. Think about the following statements (from items developed by Sessa & London, 2006). Check the statements that apply to your group.

Pressure for Change

From within the group itself, we:

☐ Face a major change in membership

☐ Have a confusing mission

☐ Feel disorganized

☐ Feel pressured by one or more members

☐ Face any other pressures from within the group:

_____

From outside the group, we:

☐ Face unrealistic expectations others may have (sponsors, stakeholders)

☐ Face significant obstacles to reaching goals

☐ Face significant pressures to get things done

☐ Have fewer resources than necessary

☐ Face other pressures from outside:

_____

Table 7.1 Ideas to Facilitate Triggers, Readiness, and Learning

Create learning triggers	• Point out opportunities. • Change goals. • Indicate barriers to goal accomplishment. • Show what competitors or other groups and organizations are doing. • Establish deadlines and rewards for meeting them.
Increase readiness to learn	• Reward new ideas and experimentation. • Provide information about other individuals, for instance, give members feedback about how other group members perceive them or encourage members to share information about their competencies so that members understand how they can best contribute to the group. • Help the group understand its progress and discuss what is working and what is not.
Support adaptive learning	• Provide information about what types of adjustments may be beneficial. • Describe models of how other groups and individuals adapted successfully.
Support generative learning	• Provide resources for learning—for instance, access to online library databases. • Give praise and other rewards (money) for learning, and be a mentor. • Allow the group the freedom to apply new knowledge and skills activities.
Support transformative learning	• Be flexible and responsive to new ideas. • Provide opportunities and resources for experimentation. • Establish a culture in the group of trying new ways of working. • Establish experiments to test the effects of changes on multiple measures that include group and individual performance and attitudes.

Readiness to Learn

In our group, we:

- ☐ Are comfortable with keeping things the way they are now
- ☐ Resist doing things differently
- ☐ Look for opportunities to learn new skills and knowledge
- ☐ Are willing to take risks on new ideas in order to find out what works
- ☐ Seek input about the team's performance from others
- ☐ Have other indicators of readiness to learn:

Our Executive Team

Shows adaptive learning:

- ☐ Keeps doing things in pretty much the same way
- ☐ Adapts when necessary
- ☐ Frequently makes small adjustments in the way the group operates
- ☐ Often tries out new things using a trial-and-error approach

Shows generative learning:

- ☐ Takes time out to figure out ways to improve our team's work processes
- ☐ Reflects on our past ways of doing things
- ☐ Seeks ideas or expertise from people external to the team
- ☐ Obtains help or advice from people external to the team
- ☐ Seeks feedback about the team's work from people external to the team
- ☐ Applies new methods to see what works

Shows transformative learning:

- ☐ Experiments with new ideas

☐ Is not afraid to do things differently from other groups

☐ Works together quite differently than it did when it first started

Other examples of adaptive, generative, and transformative learning:

High pressures for change and readiness for learning should stimulate generative and transformative learning. What pressures are your group under? Are they ready to learn? Have they learned how to adapt? Have they looked for, communicated, and applied new information, knowledge, and skills (generative learning)? Have they made any substantial changes in how they work together or what they are working on (their mission and goals)? If pressures are high but readiness to learn is low, what support do they need to increase their readiness to learn? Do you as the leader need to be more tolerant in trying out new ideas? Do you need to provide the time and resources to find new ideas even if you do not know what their value will be?

Group Learning Orientation

Some groups are high in learning orientation (Bunderson & Sutcliffe, 2003). They look for opportunities to develop new skills and knowledge, like challenging and difficult assignments that teach new things, are willing to take risks on new ideas in order to find out what works, like to work on things that require a lot of skill and ability, and see learning and developing skills as very important. Learning orientation can improve a group's performance.

Individuals as Proactive, Expansive Learners

Having individuals in your group who are high in learning orientation can increase the group's overall learning orientation. People who are high in learning orientation are *proactive learners* (Bateman

& Crant, 1993). They are constantly on the lookout for new ways to improve their lives, feel driven to make a difference in their community, and are not ones to let others take the initiative to start new projects. They are generally a powerful force for constructive change. If they see something they do not like, they fix it. They never feel constrained. Basically, they identify opportunities and act on them; they show initiative, take action, and persevere until they bring about meaningful change. Proactive learners intentionally and directly influence their situations, thereby making successful job performance more likely. They actually create situations and environments conducive to effective performance. People who are not proactive exhibit the opposite pattern. They fail to seize opportunities to initiate change.

In selecting group members, you might look for people who are high in learning orientation if you can identify them from their prior behavior. However, this might be hard to do, and more likely, you will be looking for people (or asking for volunteers) who are interested in the subject matter or have a vested interest in the group's mission. Still, you will want people who are cooperative and motivated because motivated individuals are generally willing to learn.

How Members' Learning Orientation Affects Their Willingness to Adapt to a Changing Situation

Jeffery LePine (2005), a researcher at the University of Florida, studied sixty-four three-person groups engaged in a three-hour computer-driven task. To complete this task accurately, members needed to communicate with each other. The experiment introduced a gradual breakdown in the communication channel midway through the study such that members could not send critical messages. When groups had a difficult goal, they were more likely to adapt by changing how they communicated with each other if the members were high in learning orientation—the desire to understand something novel or to increase their competence in a task. These groups focused their attention on learning about the changing situation and developing new communication strategies. These groups were more cooperative, likely to share problem-relevant information with each other, and make and evaluate suggestions about alternative ways of doing the task in light of the shifting situation. However, groups were less likely to adapt how they communicated with each other if the members were high in performance orientation—the desire to have others view their performance favorably or to avoid negative perceptions of their competence. These groups focused their attention on how they were doing relative to the goal and did not share information necessary for learning and developing appropriate new strategies.

As a group leader, you should assess group composition to understand members' learning and performance orientation. Try to shape the group's learning orientation by emphasizing the importance of learning and trying new behaviors, especially if and when the situation changes and the group appears to be stuck in its ways and does not recognize the changing demands of the situation.

Ways to Support a Group's Learning Orientation

Groups pursue learning not because individual members are inclined to be continuous learners but because the group climate fosters it. Bunderson and Sutcliffe (2003) pointed out that too much learning can compromise efficiency, especially if the group is doing well already. However, this does not mean that groups that are performing well should not seek to learn or build their competencies. These groups will be better prepared to respond to environmental changes and unanticipated challenges. A group that deliberately deemphasized learning would be embarking on a recipe for rigidity and obsolescence in the long run.

Leaders can manage the learning orientation of their group. For instance, they can determine how learning can benefit the group. Leaders can encourage members to ask questions, seek feedback, experiment, think about the results of these experiments, and discuss errors or unexpected outcomes of actions (Edmondson, 1999). Groups discover limitations in their plans when they test assumptions and raise differences of opinion openly. They need a culture of trust and safety to learn.

Learning from Fellow Group Members Makes a Group More Efficient; Learning from People Outside the Group Makes the Group More Innovative

Sze-Sze Wong (2004), working at Duke University, surveyed seventy-three work groups in different types of organizations, for instance, a financial services firm, a hospital, and a high-tech firm. She asked them how often they tried to learn from other team members and from people outside the team. The groups' managers rated their teams' efficiency and innovativeness. She found that teams whose members said they learned from each other were more efficient, and those who said they learned from people outside the group were more innovative. Cohesive groups were more likely to seek ideas outside the group, perhaps because they were comfortable in the trust they had among themselves and so were willing to go outside and share their findings with their fellow team members.

As a group leader, encourage your group members to learn from each other how to get the work done more efficiently. Also, encourage your members to look outside the group to bring in more new ideas.

Ways to Improve Group Learning

To conclude this chapter, here are some ways you can increase your group's readiness to learn:

• Visit another organization or group that has made changes recently that mirror the ones your group is trying to make. Prepare a list of questions to ask about how they got started, how they funded the change, how they managed personnel or motivational issues, leadership shifts they may have experienced, how they improved productivity, and how they communicated what they were doing to others outside the group.

• To promote adaptive learning: Think about a change your group or another group made. Discuss pressures the group was under. List the sources of these pressures. Was the group sensitive to these pressures (did they care about them)? What was needed (degree and nature of adaptation)? In what ways did the group adapt? Was this easy or hard? Were some members resistant to change? Who championed the change? Did most people accept the change readily? If not, why not? What were the sources of resistance (for example, change is difficult, a need for change was not perceived, resources did not seem to be available)? What was your role as leader in clarifying the need for change, providing the resources, and convincing members of the need for change?

• To promote generative learning: At the start of each meeting, ask members to share new information they discovered. Determine which ideas you may want to pursue. Build this discussion into the agenda. Determine which ideas you need to address later, and build these into future agendas. Be sure there is time on the agenda for each member to educate others, share information he or she has gathered, and talk about ways to use it.

• To promote transformative learning: Ask group members to think about a major change they have observed in this or other groups of which they have been a part. What major changes were made? How did they differ from what the group originally expected to happen? Who was the champion for the change (the group members, the leader, a sponsor)? Did members readily see the need for the change? Was there disagreement? If so, how was this resolved? What problems and pitfalls occurred in implementing the change, and how was each overcome?

Summary

We began this chapter by describing ways to diagnose the extent to which your group needs, and is ready, to improve. The type of learning and change the group needs depends on the pressures it is facing.

We distinguished adaptive, generative, and transformative group learning. The chapter described how events and pressures in the group's environment trigger learning. Groups vary in the extent to which they are ready to learn depending on the extent to which members are sensitive to each other and to external pressures and are able to collaborate to get work done. We described ways to support and assess group learning, build a group's learning orientation, and improve group learning over time. Here are points to remember from this chapter:

- Groups learn how to adapt, be generative, and transform.
- Adaptive learning is discovering how to make, and then making, incremental changes in response to pressures and changes in the environment.
- Generative learning is gathering new knowledge, sharing it, and finding ways to use it. This is a proactive process: the leader and group members learn how to take the initiative rather than simply respond to the environment.
- Transformative learning is making a radical shift in the group's purpose, goals, or mode of operation. Groups that transform become transformational learners who are adept at making major changes in group membership, structure, task, and goals.
- Pressures to change (from outside and within) and readiness to change (openness to new ideas, sensitivity to others) influence learning. Adaptive learning stems from external pressures. Generative and transformational learning stem from pressures and being ready to learn.
- Leaders can encourage adaptive, generative, and transformative learning. They can help the group learn to be adaptive by providing information about others' expectations, available resources, and emerging opportunities. They can help the group learn to be generative by reinforcing and rewarding acquiring new knowledge and learning new skills, sharing

that knowledge and teaching others new skills, and applying the new knowledge and skills.

- Leaders can help members determine what they learned as individuals and as a group.

- Individuals and groups vary in learning orientation. Those high in learning orientation value learning for its own sake, not its potential benefit. Leaders can support the group's continuous learning habits by being a role model for learning, providing resources for learning (for example, money to attend conferences), reinforcing learning, and establishing a culture for sharing knowledge, teaching each other, trying new things, and engaging in experiments to test the efficacy of new approaches, methods, or programs.

Chapter 8

ASSESSING YOUR GROUP'S PROGRESS AND ACHIEVEMENTS

You might wonder when and how often you should take the time to reflect on your progress and how well the group is working together. Are you accomplishing what you set out to do or what you need to do? How do other people (those outside the group) feel about your performance?

In this chapter, we show you how to recognize what group members accomplished and learned and celebrate your successes. We give you ways to determine if this was a high-performing group and whether you, the group members, and others outside the group consider the group to be successful. We suggest that as the group comes to a close, you think about the problems you faced and how you overcame them. Also, if some problems were never resolved, we offer ways to understand why and whether this limited the group. Since feedback is so important to group functioning and many leaders have trouble giving feedback to individual members and the group as a whole, we offer a primer in Appendix C.

After reading this chapter, you should be able to:

- Help your group members examine the group process and recognize what went well and what could be done better.
- Measure the performance of your group.
- Give your group members meaningful feedback, individually and for the group as a whole.

Don't Lose Sight of the Prize

This chapter is about holding things together until you finish the job, whether it is solving the problem you set out to address, making a decision, improving a work process, holding an event, achieving a sales goal, or whatever else the project or committee was about. Here we talk about energizing people to be sure the task is completed or the problem is solved, celebrating accomplishments, seeking and giving feedback about the group process, and reflecting on what you and the members of the group learned.

Periodic Reflection

Group reflection refers to members' thinking back about what they did, discussing what worked well and what went wrong, and identifying things that can be improved. Generally groups are particularly ready for this after they have accomplished a task, not when they are in the midst of it. Still, periodic reflection can be valuable, and you should consider leading a brief process analysis after each meeting.

Members do not have to wait until all their work is done to reflect on how well they are working together and improve what they are doing and how they are doing it. After a major accomplishment, or even a minor accomplishment, the group might benefit from taking a step back and reviewing what led to that success. For instance, you might ask group members what they like best about the group or what can be done to improve the way the group operates.

Ways to Encourage Reflection

After each meeting, compare your accomplishments at that meeting with the original directive you were given. Ask the group to discuss for just three or four minutes whether they feel they are closer to the directive or mission. Ask them what still has to be done to reach the mission. Ask for feedback: How was our meeting today?

Did we accomplish anything? What was the best part of the meeting? What was the worst part of the meeting? What can we do better next time as a group? Depending on how well the group members know each other, you might even ask them to provide feedback to one another about their performance that day, or they could write down comments, give them to you, and you could pass them on to the person receiving the feedback. Receiving feedback is an excellent way to assess your progress as a leader or as a group member. If you know that others will be watching your performance, you will watch it yourself as well. We say more about feedback at the end of this chapter and in Appendix C.

Reflective Groups and Innovativion

Michael A. West (2002) at the University of Sheffield in Great Britain coined the term *team reflexivity* to refer to the extent to which members discuss the group's objectives, strategies, and processes as well as the environment in which the group operates and adapts to them accordingly. Reflexivity requires three elements: (1) reflection, which includes attention, awareness, monitoring, and evaluation; (2) planning, which includes contemplating courses of actions, forming intentions, developing detailed steps for action, and examining the potential for carrying them out; and (3) action: goal-directed behaviors that are important to achieving the desired changes in the group's objectives, strategies, processes, organizations, or environments. Generally, high reflexivity occurs in groups that plan with greater detail, recognize potential problems, prioritize plans, and consider the long range as well as the short range. More detailed plans lead to greater innovation.

Coming Down to the Wire

This is the time when you are pulling all the details together and making the final push to complete your committee's or task force's work. It is time to:

- Keep group members motivated and involved to the last minute.
- Avoid burnout as the group makes the final push.
- Maximize involvement. Avoid having one or two people shoulder most of the work.

The leader of the first example in this book, the hospital quality improvement team, recognized that this was perhaps the most stressful time in the group: "We knew what we needed to do; we had the new process worked out. We just needed the energy to go the next step and try it."

Sometimes things are going well. Other times, particularly toward the end, they may seem in disarray: people fail to meet commitments, resources do not come through, costs are higher than expected, a piece of equipment breaks, and more. Indeed, the final goal may not be met, or the event may need to be postponed. (Not all groups have happy endings.) To keep things from falling to pieces at the end, here are some simple guidelines:

- Make a checklist of all final arrangements, noting dates and who is responsible. Talk to or get a report from each person.
- Remind members of the importance of the goal, its visibility, what the organization has to gain, and what they have to gain.
- Thank the members. Remind them how much the group and the organization is depending on them.
- Remember that burnout is likely; you probably will feel it yourself. Maintain accountability.

Now your goal is to prepare the final report, make the last presentation, or hold the final event. Focus on your objectives, and do not let unimportant issues distract you or the group.

Concluding the Group

The last phase of group development is adjourning. As the group comes to a conclusion, members can celebrate their successes, reflect on what they learned, and plan for the future.

Reflecting on Group Process and Outcomes

If the task has been completed successfully, the last meeting is likely to be a good time for the members to think about how the group members worked together, what they learned about themselves and how they interacted, and the need for someone (group members, perhaps, or some other authority) to track the continued success or value of the group's outcome and make adjustments if need be. Essentially this is a postmortem. The chair of the committee or task force may need to build this into the agenda and be sure the group has ample time to assess its process and products.

Groups are likely to peter out after an activity or event has been held, something has been produced, or a decision has been made. The group members may feel exhausted—burned out, really—and be just as happy to forget the ordeal. This is especially likely if the group had trouble achieving its goals or group members had to work particularly hard to make it all happen.

Perhaps the group did not reach a successful conclusion. The special event may have attracted a disappointingly small audience, something may have gone wrong, or members may have come to dislike each other after all the arguing. Still, taking the time to reflect on the process and give each other a pat on the back (if deserved) and discuss lessons learned can be valuable.

Seeking and Giving Feedback

Members can give each other feedback about the group as a whole. This can be easier to give and take than giving individuals feedback. Individual feedback from the leader or fellow group members can be threatening, of course. However, people often want this type of feedback and will ask for it; they do not necessarily want to enhance their self-image by praise but rather seek to verify what they know about themselves—their strengths and their weaknesses. That is, they want group members to rely on their strengths and recognize their weaknesses so they will not be expected to do something they cannot or do not want to do. Leaders can promote the give-and-take of individual feedback by asking members to give them feedback about their leadership of the committee or task force. They can also ask members to self-nominate for different tasks—for example, "Who wants to help with the data analysis?" or "Who would be good to collect the data?" Discussing task assignments is a way for members to express their interests and capabilities and be sure other members heard them correctly.

Since a committee or task force is short-lived, the leader may feel that there is no need to give members feedback when the effort has ended. Certainly they should be thanked, as we emphasize next. However, this is also a time to recognize the members' strengths by summarizing what each person did well. Of course, the leader should have been giving frequent, specific feedback to the group all along, and this would have ensured that the members were aware of problems they encountered (or even caused). There is no need to harp on what went wrong. The members will probably be well aware of this themselves. The chair of the fundraising committee might say to the members who arranged the catering, "Roberto and Sheila did an outstanding job working with the caterer. They planned the menus; organized the timing of the event; determined the seating, which had its own set of politics; and ensured that we had enough staff on hand for coat checks and valet parking. They left no detail unturned." Note that the chair was specific about what behaviors Roberto and Sheila did well. He did not just say, "We appreciate Roberto and Sheila's work with the caterer." Their forte, apparently, is organizing complex tasks, and the chair and other committee members should remember that for the next event. The chair might also ask Roberto and Sheila to write a guide for future committees, listing the tasks that need to be done and the problems to look out for. Roberto or Sheila might have had trouble on other tasks, for instance, they might not have recruited many people to attend the event. But the chair might have expected everyone to recruit some attendees. Of course, Roberto and Sheila were not the only ones responsible for this, and maybe arranging for catering is not the sort of thing they like to do. Being specific about members' behaviors and strengths that led to accomplishments gives them feedback that helps them understand themselves better and is a reward in and of itself. (Appendix C has more information about feedback.)

Acknowledging and Thanking Group Members

A thank-you is always appropriate. It is especially important after the group has accomplished a major task. All contributors should be acknowledged. This seems obvious, but it is easy to ignore, especially in the aftermath of a difficult project. The group as a whole can take credit (for example, "This wouldn't have happened without us") and be recognized by others (an executive might say, "This committee did outstanding work!"). However, the chair should be sure that each person is recognized publicly.

Celebrating Success

Your group has come to the end. Even before you do a debriefing to reflect on what went right and wrong and review what the group and each of the members learned, we recommend celebrating your success:

- Thank group members for their contributions.
- Recognize outstanding performance.
- Maintain everyone's interest long enough to do a debriefing.
- Encourage members to be involved in the future in this or other groups.
- Help other groups by spreading the word about your group's accomplishments and how they were achieved.
- Help group members recognize what they learned and how to apply it to other groups.

To provide another case example, after a corporate task force designed and implemented a new enterprise-wide data system (a two-year, $11 million project), the company sponsored a bash for everyone involved. The idea of the party was not to say, "This is fair recompense for all your extra time and effort," but rather simply to acknowledge that everyone did work hard, that the outcome was a success, and that they needed to relax a bit and feel good about it. Members of the task force received one-time bonuses in their paychecks at the end of the year—sizable bonuses that were in line with their accomplishments. In addition, some members of the task force submitted a proposal to a professional conference about what they had done. This was accepted, and the company supported the members' trip to the conference. Of course, this exposure was just as good for the company as it was for the careers of the individuals involved.

In the hospital quality improvement team example from Chapter One, the team members participated in a local conference of other quality improvement teams. Descriptions of the different teams' activities and accomplishments were displayed on posters, similar to a science conference. The efforts were judged by hospital administrators, and the team in our example won an award for most significant improvement.

Measuring Your Group's Performance

There are different ways to measure group outcomes. Some are objective—for instance, Was the goal accomplished? Were deadlines met? Improvements made? Money saved?

You can also measure elements of group process. How long did the group take? Did it take longer than expected or less time? Did achieving the goal cost more or less than expected, or was it right on budget? Did members meet commitments? Did they stay with the committee, or was there a lot of unanticipated turnover as people quit midstream?

You can also measure performance subjectively. Basically, how did sponsors and stakeholders feel about the group's efforts and outcomes? How did you feel as the group leader? How did members feel? How would you evaluate your group on the following qualities (adapted from Hirschfeld, Jordan, Field, & Armenakis, 2005):

Group Members' Confidence in Their Capacity to Perform Well

- My group believes it can be very productive.
- My group has confidence in itself.
- No task is too tough for my group.
- My group expects to be known as a high-performing group.

Group Unity and Trust

- My group has a strong sense of togetherness.
- My group members trust one another.
- My group lacks team spirit (or the reverse).
- My group members agree on our goals.

Group Proficiency

- My group accomplishes our goals.
- My group meets deadlines.
- My group produces high-quality work.
- My group lets problems fester (or the reverse).

Observed Teamwork

- My group members are committed to helping each other.
- My group members participate actively during group meetings.
- My group members communicate well.
- My group does not waste time.
- My group members take advantage of each other's expertise.

You also can ask, "Was this a high-performing group?" (see the discussion in Chapter Two). Then evaluate each of the three components of a high-performing group:

- *Talent:* Group members have the capabilities and motivation.
- *Time:* Deadlines are met.
- *Task:* Objectives, methods, and assessment methods are clear.

Recognizing What *You* Learned About Leading

Throughout this book, we have tried to make the process of leading a small, temporary group less daunting than you might think. We have offered ideas that will help you start out positively and stay on track.

When you are appointed to lead a committee or task force, you need to diagnose the situation—both what you are facing and the people you will be working with. What are the issues? How do the members feel about being part of the group? Have they worked together before?

Next, you now know how groups usually develop over time: how they get to know one another, express their different perspectives, settle on common goals, and establish how they are going to work together to achieve these goals. You know that groups often shift from floundering to settling on a path and getting the work done.

As the leader, you shape this process by (1) the people you select for the group; (2) how you define and structure the task's objectives, work methods, and methods for assessment of progress and outcomes; and (3) the time lines you set. How the group evolves depends on the competencies, experiences, motivation, and personalities of the group members. It will also depend on the expectations and goals that others have for your group (your sponsor or stakeholders) and the resources available. If your group is like most others, you will face a variety of external pressures: high expectations, tough goals to reach, and tight resources. Only rarely will you have all the money and time you need and no real objectives or deadlines.

You now know how to think about your own style of leadership and the needs of the group. You might like to control the situation and call all the shots, but you realize that the reason for the group is that the job is too big for one person. Other people have expertise that you lack or need to buy into whatever the group is doing. So you consider how to vary your behavior to fit the situation. Indeed, leadership is a balancing act between finding a common group goal and recognizing members' vested interests, desire to call the shots, and expectations that they will participate actively, responding to pressures to get work done and having time to think about what you are doing. You need to worry about the details and create and be a champion for a vision that everyone on your group can rally around.

As the group begins its work, you set the stage for a positive group climate. Members get to know one another and what they can expect from each other. Icebreakers help members feel comfortable working together. They develop the confidence that they can handle the task by working collaboratively.

Now you know how to improve the group process as it evolves. Find someone on or off the group who can be a sounding board for ideas and a source of advice. You may work with a group facilitator who can train the group in using a variety of structured processes. You learn how to handle difficult members and other sources of possible dysfunction.

As you progress, you recognize that you, the individual members of your group, and the group as a whole are learning. You are learning how to adapt to pressures inside and outside the group. You are learning to be generative, discovering new information, acquiring knowledge and skills, sharing them with the group, and experimenting with new ways to apply them. You may be learning how to transform yourselves into a very different group from when you started—a group with a new purpose, goals, work methods, and maybe even members. In the process, you hone your readiness to learn, including your openness to new ideas and concepts and your sensitivity to others' concerns and values.

End your experience as a group leader by reflecting on what you learned about yourself as a leader and about your group. Ask your group members, sponsors, stakeholders, and observers (perhaps a facilitator or someone you consider to be your coach) for feedback. Think mindfully about the feedback and what it means to you. Then address the question of what you would do differently the next time you lead a group.

To help you out in this process, you might ask an objective party, perhaps someone who was not part of the group, to collect feedback from your group members and summarize the results. You could meet with that person to discuss what he or she learned about your leadership role in this group. We recommend discussing the results with the group members to clarify what they meant. Having the objective party's report is an icebreaker. Individual group members will not be identified by name. Sharing the report or key findings with the group will expand their trust in you for future interactions and provide a basis for discussion that is not threatening to you or the members who provided the information.

Feedback works the other way around as well. Members may want feedback from you. You can certainly give the group as a whole feedback in the group setting. Provide your insights and observation as their leader. Say what they did well and might have done better. Do not name names or insinuate that certain people were responsible for certain negative outcomes. Be general, and keep the discussion focused on the group level. Meet with group members privately to give them individual feedback.

Be sure to evaluate both outcomes (what was accomplished) and process (how the group brought about these outcomes).

Areas for feedback and discussion can focus on the following:

- Questions about you as the leader: Goal clarity, communication, fairness, listening, involving group members in making decisions (democratic), organized, reflective, flexible
- Questions about the group: Feeling comfortable, effectiveness, efficiency, mutual respect, ability to resolve conflicts, psychological safety

- Questions about each other: Met commitments, contributed knowledge and expertise, willing to help out, contributed actively to discussions

Here are some samples of quotes from leaders and group members. These are the kind of statements you might hear that you will want to explore in a wrap-up group meeting:

About the Leader

"She always listened to us."

"He pushed too hard."

"He was very organized. We always had a clear agenda, but we never got through it."

"We spent too much time early on hashing and rehashing ideas. It wasn't until we were two weeks from our deadline that we got moving. He could have saved us a lot of time and aggravation."

About the Group as a Whole

"We really turned this around."

"We were all dedicated."

"Let's face it: most of us didn't have our hearts in this."

"This was a wonderful experience. I learned a lot and got to know some terrific people."

"This turned out to be more work than any of us expected. We bit off more than we could chew."

To measure what the group learned and the extent to which the group learned to be adaptive, generative, or transformative (see Chapter Seven for the definition of these types of learning), ask yourself and the group members the following:

Adaptive Learning

To what extent did our group:

- Learn how to work together as a single unit?
- Learn how to perform its tasks?
- Learn to adapt to changing conditions?
- Gain knowledge of and use each member's capabilities?
- Learn to be flexible?

Generative Learning

To what extent did our group:

- Learn new skills and behaviors?
- Acquire new knowledge?
- Bring new information to the group?
- Learn different ways to accomplish our mission and goals?
- Learn how to find resources?
- Learn from each other?

Transformative Learning

To what extent did our group:

- Purposefully restructure in response to outside pressures?
- Form new alliances with other groups?
- Create something new?
- Demonstrate that we were capable of doing whatever it took to succeed?
- Show that we were able to change in the face of emergencies and unexpected demands?

Overall Performance of Our Group

To what extent did our group:

- Meet our goals?
- Accomplish the tasks we set out to do?
- Meet our own needs and expectations?
- Work well as a unit?
- Burn out our members?

Additional Reflection

- Describe any unusual circumstances that the group had to deal with.
- Describe how this group compared to others you have been on.
- Overall, how effective was the group in accomplishing the goals?
- How efficient was the group in terms of its performance?
- How innovative was the group in terms of its performance?
- What was a major success of the group?
- What were major difficulties or barriers the group needed to overcome?
- What would you do differently next time you are asked to chair a committee?
- What did you learn about yourself?
- What could you (or did you) say to the group as a whole about how things worked?

Suggestions for Facilitating Group Reflection

- Ask members these questions and have them write a two-minute essay as feedback to you, or go round robin.
- Write each member a thank-you note. Indicate what you especially valued about his or her contribution to the group. If there was something negative, add that you would be happy to talk to the person privately. Do not be critical in the note. Let the person come to you if he or she is interested.

- Keep a record of the group. You might want to send your letter and a summary description of each individual's performance to the person's supervisor if this is a work situation or add the information to the person's personnel file. If this is a volunteer organization, you might want to keep records of the positive contributions each person made so you will know whom to call on in the future.

- Talk about the extent to which the group is a repository of knowledge. What knowledge? Who has it? How can it be used in the future?

Remember that assessing and reflecting on your progress is important for you as a leader and the group. Feedback can help you improve the group process and improve as a leader of future groups. As you celebrate your group's success, recognize the mistakes you might have made and will try not to repeat. And do not forget the actions you took that worked, perhaps to your surprise and delight!

Now you're ready for your next leadership experience. Congratulations!

Summary

Assessment is a key aspect of leading a group, and it should be done not just at the end, but all along the way. Groups do better when they take time to reflect on what is happening. This helps them get energized, focus on the tasks they need to accomplish, and eventually capture what they learned. As the group comes down to the wire, you need to sustain their excitement and get ready to celebrate success. In the course of measuring and reviewing each individual member's contributions and the performance of the group as a whole, recognize what you learned about leadership and what you might do differently next time. Remember the following:

- Help group members reflect on their progress. Guide your group in stepping back to think about how well members are working together.

- Maintain momentum and motivation as the group comes closer to completing its tasks and meeting its goals. Then get ready to celebrate success, measure performance, and provide feedback to individuals or the group as a whole, depending on the group's focus on individual or group goals.

- Learn how to give meaningful individual and group feedback (see the primer on feedback in Appendix C).

We conclude with eight major guidelines—one from each step in the process of leading a group:

1. Determine the type of group you are leading and what this means for you as a leader (Chapter One).

2. Structure talent, time, and task as keys to a high-performing group (Chapter Two).

3. Recognize and plan for stages of development (Chapter Three).

4. Create balance, and practice different leadership roles, such as communicator, builder of trust, and facilitator (Chapter Four).

5. Get off to an effective start quickly; be sure members know one another's potential contributions (Chapter Five and Appendix A).

6. Promote teamwork, generate collective efficacy, and use conflict resolution and negotiation strategies (Chapter Six and Appendix B).

7. Use adaptive, generative, or transformative learning strategies to improve your group's performance (Chapter Seven).

8. Assess process and outcomes; seek and give feedback (Chapter Eight and Appendix C).

Appendix A
QUICK START GUIDE

Getting started requires preparation and setup before the first meeting even begins. This guide reflects the ideas of Fred Niziol and Kathy Free, professional facilitators who outlined a structured group start-up process. Their approach starts with thinking about issues that the group may confront, preparing the first agenda, and considering how to establish ground rules for how the group will operate (Niziol & Free, 2005). We draw from and extend their approach to suggest steps for getting your group started and keeping it on track. You may have a professional group facilitator to work with or perhaps a supervisor or experienced group member (perhaps a past president of the organization) with whom you can consult.

Group Start-Up Process

Advance Planning

- Consider each of the following as you plan for your group.

    Are there potential problems and sensitive issues and challenges?

    Plan the first agenda, work methods, responsibilities for materials and facilities setup, and your role (how you will address the group, explain your expectations, and manage the group process).

    Consider how group members will communicate in between meetings (for example, conference calls, e-mail,

237

an online blog). Be sure you and committee members have the needed technology and know-how to accommodate these alternative modes of communication, and consider the extent to which these communications methods lessen the need for in-person meetings and increase communication efficiency.

- If you are able to work with a professional facilitator, meet with that individual before the first meeting to discuss issues and plan the agenda, methods, and leadership roles.

  Discuss with the facilitator ground rules for how you will work together (for example, meet before and after each meeting, determine when the facilitator will provide group members with training in group process techniques, agree on what the facilitator will do during meetings).

Room Preparation

- Prepare flip charts, paper, markers, tape, name or tent cards, and copies of information about the group's project.
- Prepare a flip chart with a page labeled "Parking Lot" for ideas, action items, and possible solutions. Explain that this will be used to record issues that come up and are important but inappropriate for the current discussion and that the group will review it periodically.
- If you expect to break out into smaller groups, identify breakout rooms and prepare materials for each room.

First Meeting Agenda

- Welcome members.
- Provide general housekeeping (information about breaks and ending times, locations of rest rooms, roster of group members or attendance sheet, name tags).
- Introduce group members. For example, ask each member to tell the group about a special interest, hobby, or something about him or her that others might not guess as a way of intro-

ducing common ground but does not reveal the person's position or role in the organization yet.

- Explain the history of the group, its purpose, and expectations.
- Introduce the facilitator and say that he or she will provide training when needed.
- Consider using an icebreaker to help members feel comfortable with each other. (See Chapter Six for examples.)
- Distinguish between and define the group's purpose or mission, its intended product or outcome, and the group's process (how members will work together and make decisions to achieve the outcome).
- Clarify the group's purpose.

   Exercise: Read the stem of a statement such as the following and go around the room, asking members to complete the statement; record responses on a flip chart:

   To focus on mission, say, "I believe our group has been asked to . . ."

   To focus on agenda, say, "In today's meeting, I hope we will . . ."

   To focus on operating procedures, say, "I expect our group to complete its work in . . . months."

- Explain consensus decision making and practice this during the start-up.

   Explain ways of achieving consensus. Define consensus as the process of asking members if they support a proposal and, if not, whether they can live with it. The group then works toward a solution that all members can support. This stresses the cooperative development of a decision with group members working together rather than competing against each other.

   Exercise: Ask one person to clearly state a decision, ask another to record it, ask others if this is correct, and get clarification. When consensus is agreed, write "agreed by consensus" and the date next to the item on the flip chart.

- Discuss other ways to make decisions and when you might use them (for example, motion and voting, majority or two-thirds majority vote). Recognize that when groups vote, there are winners and losers. Strive for consensus, and use majority rule vote when consensus does not seem possible or to demonstrate and formally record the level of agreement.

- Establish ground rules and operating procedures: responsibilities, meeting schedules, logistics for future meetings, rules (for example, for calling on members, making decisions), starting times for meetings and how to handle people who are absent or late, whether the group will make decisions even if someone is absent, how minutes will be taken and circulated.

- Elect or appoint and review group roles: group leader, meeting leader, minute taker, timekeeper.

- Establish group member interests and concerns. Have members answer and discuss responses to the following: "It's important to me that the group succeed because . . ." or "My concerns about the group project are . . ."

- Describe brainstorming: members express ideas, record the ideas on a flip chart, but do not evaluate the ideas.

- Discuss how to evaluate and consolidate ideas after brainstorming.

- Explain multivoting to prioritize ideas or issues: divide the total number of items by three; this is the number of votes each person has to distribute.

- Create a vision. Have members respond to the following: "We'll know this group has succeeded when . . ." or "If we did a great job, what would we have done?" Record answers on a flip chart.

- Develop a mission statement: purpose, scope, time we can devote to the work per week, whom we are doing the work for, how the group will present the results, whether the group has the needed skills and resources, and what the members will see if the group is successful.

- Draft a work plan for arranging meetings, collecting data, preparing status reports, identifying times and methods for monthly reviews, and distributing the pilot group's recommendations.

- Review alternative means of communications among meetings (for example, e-mail, instant messaging, telephone) and virtual meetings (for example, telephone conference calls, online and Web meetings in combination with telephone conference calls, chatrooms, teleconferences of subgroups that are geographically apart meeting separately with a telephone or video hookup).

- Plan for the next meeting.

- Process check. Brainstorm what went well, what the group liked about the meeting, and what needs improvement.

- Thank the group for its hard work.

You may progress through most of these steps quickly, maybe all during the first meeting, or you may need several meetings.

Possible Items for the Second Meeting

- Read minutes from the previous meeting, ask for clarifications and corrections, and approve the minutes.

- Starting with the mission as a point of reference, identify objectives. The objectives may be different projects or activities the group will conduct in order to accomplish its overall mission. Objectives may be different ways to accomplish the mission. They should be expressed as outcomes or actions that are specific and measurable, that is, you can determine whether they were accomplished and measure how well. Note that members of your group may not have had written objectives before. Use our learning objectives at the start of each chapter in this book as a model for how to write specific, measurable objectives.

- If the mission and objective are the same, discuss different ways the objective can be carried out or different tasks that need to be carried out in order to accomplish it. Use brainstorming to identify the objectives. Alternatively, pair the group members to write objectives, and then bring the whole group together for a discussion. Prioritize the objectives. Which ones are essential, and which are less important? Ask the group to vote to select the top three. Decide which objectives you will work on to accomplish the group's mission. Be sure the objectives you choose are reachable within your deadline.

- Ask members to select objectives that they would like to work on, and begin researching information for the next meeting.

Subsequent Meeting

- Ask members to share what they learned about the objectives they chose.

- Make final decisions about who will work on each objective. Create subgroups and ask members to discuss alternative plans for meeting their objective. Have them report their ideas back to the whole group to get feedback.

- *Group assignment:* Based on the feedback and what was accomplished in this meeting, develop a plan for how you will accomplish the objective you chose or were assigned. Bring your plan to the next group meeting to share with the group.

- Sometimes multiple members have to work on one objective. Be sure that members have contact information so they can communicate between meetings.

- Have individuals or small groups report their plans to the whole group. Depending on what your group is doing, each plan could take a whole meeting or two or three.

- Discuss the plans, revise them, and then prioritize them.

- Create a timetable for how the group will proceed. Decide what steps will be needed to complete the mission, and create deadlines for each step.
- Set up a follow-up meeting for each deadline to review the progress of the group.
- Talk about indicators of success. How will the group know they have achieved their goals? How will they assess degree of success? Who else will evaluate their success?

Between Meetings

- Provide resources.
- Stay in touch with group members so you can see how the work is progressing. You may decide to move the next meeting up or back depending on what you learn as you talk to members between meetings.
- Touch base with your supervisor for clarification of your charge, additional resources, or more information as the project progresses. If there is any reason you think the group may not make the deadline, you should explain why, ask for help, or ask if the deadline can be extended. Be honest. Do not surprise your supervisor or constituents with unexpected news. This reflects poorly on you and your group members.

Follow-Up Meetings

- Ask each individual or small group to report to the whole group on what they have accomplished. Ask the group for feedback, and discuss the comments. Decide what will be kept and what must be changed. Based on the original time line, decide on a deadline for the change to be completed. Revisit the change before the deadline so the task can be completed on time or even early.
- Be flexible. As the group progresses, you may have to change some objectives, the time line, your players, or something else. Always keep the mission and the project deadline in mind.

Final Meetings

- Prepare to produce the objectives. An objective might have been to conduct a study and present the results, produce a plan and describe it, make a recommendation or decision, or hold an event or activity. In all cases, the last meetings of the group will address bringing everything together to generate the final outcome.

- If a presentation is involved, decide how the results or project will be presented and who the audience is. The way the information is presented should reflect who will be listening and what the message is. Consider how many members of the group should be present, the method of presentation (visuals, audios, workshops, demonstrations), how long the presentation should be to keep the attention of the audience, and whether the presentation should be passive or active in terms of what the audience will do. When the presentation is given, consider the following suggestions:

  > Be sure all group members know where and when to go on the day of the presentation, as well as what to bring and what to do.

  > Keep the presentation to the time allotted for it.

  > Ask for feedback, and listen carefully to what is said.

  > Ask one member of the group to take notes on the discussion that ensues and report back to the group with a summary.

  > Plan what the group will do in the future if the intention is to keep the group intact. Make plans for future directions.

Close the Group

- Ask the group to meet after the presentation, activity, or announcement.

- Review the criteria for success that the group established during the first or second meeting. Were time lines met? What were the results of the evaluation measures—for instance, how people reacted to the presentation, the number of people who attended the event, or reactions to the announced decision or recommendations?

- Ask for feedback about your leadership skills, as well as how the group did.
- What can you do better next time?

Focus on Talent, Task, and Time

As we said in Chapter Three, talent, task, and time are the building blocks of a high-performing group. Use the following guidelines to facilitate the development of each of these elements as the group process unfolds:

1. Be sure that members have the skills, knowledge, and abilities needed for the work of the group.

    Recruit members with the needed skills.

    Ask members what they can do for the group. This may not be obvious to you or the individuals themselves at first. Some people may have volunteered for the group because their friend volunteered, or they were assigned to the group and had little choice in the matter.

    Integrate new members into the group: introduce them, explain why they are there, and make them feel comfortable and welcome.

2. Be sure the members are clear about the group's goals from the start.

    Explain the purpose of the group.

    State your vision.

    Ask members for their vision.

    Form a group vision to which all members are committed.

Ask members to decide what the key questions would be to guide their decisions, policies, and actions. Perhaps ask members to agree on how they would finish this question as a guide against which to evaluate decisions: "Does this decision . . . ?"

Develop expectations and standards for evaluating individuals' contributions to the group.

3. At the first meeting, explain the importance of the task:

Explain how the group product will be used and why it is important to the group, the organization, or others.

Provide examples of how the group's work will be used.

Explain who will benefit from the group's work.

4. Be sure members know each other well enough early on so that they now understand how each person could contribute to the group.

At the first meeting, ask members to introduce themselves. Have them describe their background.

Consider asking members to tell something about their lives, such as where they grew up, how many siblings they have, where they went to school, and whether they are married and have children. The purpose is to help members identify with each other and see what they have in common. Some people may not want to provide personal information. Ask them what information they would feel comfortable sharing so that they can get to know each other better.

5. Be sure members have the time they need to devote to the task.

Inform members how much time you expect them to have available to work on the group's task. Be sure they are able to attend all, or at least most, group meetings and they have other time available to do whatever needs to be done outside the meetings.

If members indicate that they have other time pressures, speak to their supervisor to decrease their other responsibilities. You may need to replace members who do not have sufficient time. Finding this out at the outset is best.

6. Be sure members have a clear idea about their roles.

How the task will be done and each member's role may not be clear from the outset. Also, members may want to work on determining how the work will get done and what their roles will be. Let them know that this will be part of what you will do early on. That way, their expectations will be clear, and they will feel confident that you will listen and act on their ideas.

If the path to accomplishing the group's goals is clear from the start and members are waiting for you to structure the task for them, then be specific. Explain who you want to do what and by when. Be precise in making assignments and setting deadlines. Alternatively, you may want the group to make these decisions instead of your assigning them. If so, group consensus on who does what is essential so that everyone understands their responsibilities to the group.

Set the dates and times for meetings after getting information about members' availability. Explain what you will do at each meeting. Having an agenda and minutes will be useful.

7. Be sure deadlines are clear. Track whether the group is meeting deadlines.

Set deadlines for each major element of the group's work.

Set a deadline for the group's finished product. Monitor the product at each deadline, and be sure guidelines for assessment are clear from the onset.

If deadlines are not met or it seems as if the group will not meet a deadline, do something about it before the deadline passes, or give the group more time. Do not let the deadline go by without comment. Celebrate meeting deadlines. Be sure members know that deadlines are important; otherwise, they will not take them seriously.

8. Facilitate group progress.

> Ask the group to evaluate its own progress. Hold discussions about how things are working and what can be done differently to improve group progress.
>
> Get everyone's thoughts about ways to improve group progress.
>
> Measure your progress against standards and expectations that you establish at the start of the group so that feedback is specific and occurs frequently and at expected times.

9. Measure and recognize goal accomplishments.

> Celebrate achieving goals. Goals may be milestones along the way to a final objective. Milestones help the group track progress, recognize what still needs to get done, and plan their work to meet their goals.
>
> Ask the group members to evaluate group accomplishments. As the leader, state your view of how well the group did. Gather information from others outside the group, particularly those who use the work of the group (clients, customers, other groups).

10. Build pride in group accomplishments.

> Reward group accomplishments. Recognize individual members who made outstanding contributions. Recognize the group as a whole for its excellent work.
>
> Be sure group members know that you, as the leader, are proud of the group's efforts and results.

Appendix B

NEGOTIATION AND CONFLICT RESOLUTION STRATEGIES

Early group meetings are the time to set the stage for raising and resolving conflicts and negotiating constructively. Of course, not all decisions involve conflict, and as the leader, you want open discussion. The storming stage of group development, which may occur more than once during the life of a group, is the process of working through any disagreements, different viewpoints, and conflicts about what the group is going to do.

Getting Members to Reach Agreement

A reason that people disagree is that they have different perspectives—different vested interests, information, or burning concerns. They have their own goals, which may be separate from, or sometimes the inverse of, what the group is trying to do. In the example of the building location committee for the food pantry from Chapter Seven, the restaurant owner did not want the pantry near her restaurant. She admitted as much to the committee chair before the group even started meeting, although she never voiced this concern out loud to the group. She just kept evaluating every idea in relation to her own objective. After several unproductive meetings with this member spending a good part of each meeting going on and on about why one idea after another would not work, other members stopped coming to the meetings. Actually, the other committee members were quite respectful of this member even though she did not really deserve it. Perhaps they felt that she was an important person in town, and in any case, several of the members worked together actively on the town's chamber of commerce, so perhaps they did not want to confront her. The situation changed when the group started a new tactic: listing and questioning assumptions and exploring a wide range of alternatives for each need. The brainstorming mode required that each person participate without evaluating others' ideas when they were raised.

How to Resolve Conflicts

Conflict is not necessarily a bad thing. In fact, it is fairly natural and can be constructive if it is managed well. It can lead to innovation and new ways of thinking. However, people often are stubborn. They get mired in narrow ways of thinking. Consider the following ways to turn adversaries into allies:

- Do not shy away from conflict. Help your group recognize their different points of view.
- Focus on one conflict at a time. Do not try to do too much. Break the problem or issue into components.
- Do not react negatively to unintentional remarks. Focus on what is important.
- Consider timing. If people are too emotional, wait until everyone calms down. This might mean waiting until the next meeting.
- Avoid personalizing the conflict. Name-calling, threats, and blame never work.
- Agree to disagree.
- Find common ground that you agree on.
- As the leader, remain neutral. Clarify perspectives and assumptions. Emphasize that you recognize the differences in opinion and that you are trying to be objective and open to understanding these differences.
- Maintain communication. Ask open-ended questions. Be an active listener. Repeat what others are saying so they realize

that you understand. Then summarize, reframe, and reflect on the areas of disagreement and agreement.

- Do not focus on an area of agreement and assume prematurely that all is resolved. As you move forward in the discussion, clarify changes in opinion or note that some members seem willing to defer to others' opinions, perhaps for the good of the group.

There are five ways to resolve conflict (Kilman & Thomas, 1975):

1. *Compete:* Members keep pushing for their issue and do not give up the fight easily, if at all, until they "win." They are firm in pursuing their goals, and they want to win their position using any means. This is likely when individuals feel passionately about an issue and place little value on interpersonal relationships in the group.

2. *Accommodate:* Members go along with each other. They may not agree, but they are willing to express their viewpoint and then defer to others. They are considerate of each other's wishes and try not to hurt each other's feelings, even if it means letting things they disagree about go by. This happens when members value relationships and do not feel they have a strong personal stake in the issue.

3. *Avoid:* Members ignore areas about which they feel they will disagree. If disagreements crop up, they stop talking about them and move on to something else. They avoid taking positions that will create controversy, and let others take the responsibility for solving a problem. The result is that some important decisions may not get made. This happens when members do not care very much about the issue or about each other's feelings, but they are unwilling to invest personal energy one way or the other.

4. *Compromise:* Members identify ways of resolving issues on which they disagree. They recognize each other's viewpoints

and agree to give in partially. They give a little and get a little. This is similar to collaboration except that members do not change their viewpoints or create new viewpoints. This is most likely when members have a reasonable, but not overly strong, personal stake in the issue and they respect, and care about, one another and want to maintain positive working and social relationships among the group members.

5. *Collaborate:* Members express their personal views, listen to each other, repeat each other's concerns to be sure they understand the differences in viewpoint and other members realize they do, and then find common ground. They attempt to get all concerns and issues immediately out in the open, and seek each other's help in working out solutions to problems. This happens when members care strongly about the issue and also care about and respect each other.

Conflict Resolution Exercise

Try this exercise to reach consensus. When an issue arises, identify a group member to represent each viewpoint. Ask each representative to list areas of agreement on a flip chart. In doing so, they may see more agreement than disagreement and realize the area of disagreement is not important. List the opposing viewpoints. Ask the representative from each viewpoint to express it and write it down on the flip charts. Contrast the opposing views to identify the central areas of disagreements to get at the heart of the matter. Ask a third party, perhaps another group member who has not taken a side, to list possible compromises. Write down the compromises. Examine the pros and cons of each (for example, cost, time). Then list all the alternatives. Ask the group to multivote (for example, spread ten points across alternatives). See which ones have the most votes. Is there a clear winner? If not, consider inviting one or more third parties (a supervisor or group sponsor) to decide.

Avoiding Conflict

Here are some ideas to avoid defensiveness and prevent conflicts from arising (adapted from Robin & Foster, 2003):

- Instead of accusing, blaming, and being defensive, make "I" statements, for instance, "I feel . . . when . . . happens."
- Instead of talking in the third person about someone who is in the room, talk directly to the person.
- Instead of putting fellow members down, accept responsibility.
- Instead of interrupting, listen and encourage speakers to use brief statements.
- Instead of overgeneralizing, making extreme statements, or making situations sound like catastrophes or disasters, use qualifying statements, such as "sometimes" or "maybe," and try to be as accurate as possible.
- Instead of lecturing, preaching, or moralizing, make brief, explicit problem statements, such as, "I would like . . ."
- Instead of speaking in a sarcastic tone of voice, speak in a neutral tone.
- Instead of failing to make eye contact, look at the person with whom you are speaking.
- Instead of fidgeting, moving restlessly, arms folded in front of chest or gesturing while being spoken to, sit in a relaxed fashion, arms down, hands open or folded up in your lap.
- Instead of saying what you believe others think, ask them to state their viewpoints themselves.
- Instead of getting off topic or dwelling on the past, catch yourself and return to the problem at hand.
- Instead of commanding, ordering, or threatening, suggest alternative solutions.
- Instead of intellectualizing, speak in simple, clear language.

- Instead of humoring fellow members or discounting what they say, be reflective and thoughtful, and validate their statements—for instance, "I see what you mean," or "So you are saying . . ."

- Instead of monopolizing the conversation, be sure everyone takes turns making brief statements.

- Instead of remaining silent rather than responding, express your negative feelings and disagreements.

Negotiating Consensus (Not Compromise) and Managing Conflict

Consensus is not compromise. Compromise implies giving in. With consensus, everyone agrees that one decision is the best. The question then becomes, Can everyone in the group come to a consensus about which decision is the best one? Moving from compromise to consensus is essential. It avoids later resentment that might result from feeling that you gave in.

In their classic book *Getting to Yes: Negotiating Agreement Without Giving In* (1991), Roger Fisher, William Ury, and Bruce Patton outlined methods for what they call "principled negotiation." These principles apply to group interaction. Consider that decisions made in a group are like a series of mini-negotiations between group members. Negotiating agreement requires focusing on the merits of an argument, not on people, and finding a goal that allows all parties to win to some degree. Avoid attacking others' positions and defending your own position since this tends to lock you into having to support a position. Remember that when you are working in a group, your objective is to have all the group members work together toward a common goal.

To clarify all points of view, try using our suggestion above for recording areas of agreement and disagreement on a flip chart. Then consider the merits of each idea. Find out more about each member's reasoning, and listen carefully. The goal is for the group members to model your behavior and listen too. Review (perhaps list) the pros and cons of each viewpoint. Ask questions rather than make statements that cause others to be defensive.

Consider what your best alternative would be to each solution that your members bring to the table. You might even consider what you will do if the solution you hope for is not brought up at the meeting or is not supported at the meeting. Fisher, Ury, and Patton (1991) call this the "best alternative to a negotiated agreement." You do not have to disclose your best alternative to the group. Let others come up with it if you can. If you cannot improve the direction in which the group moves, consider stopping the discussion and moving to another topic, delaying the decision (which may slow down your group's progress), or finding an alternative that had not been considered before.

The idea of having a best alternative in a group setting is to be able to bring the group back to the charge and the objectives, or even to have an alternative set of objectives to consider if the first set does not work out. One of the most important concepts of negotiation is to avoid shutting down communication. After all, you want to maintain positive relationships in the group. If communication breaks down, so will the group's ability to work together, and you will never finish your work.

As an example, consider a committee that is determining ways to allocate a sum of money. Everyone seems to have a different opinion about how to use the funds. Your view as committee chair is that the best alternative to not reaching an agreement about what to do with the money is to split the money fifty-fifty: half to any project the majority wants and the other half to savings for a rainy day fund. After considerable discussion, a member suggests splitting the money in multiple ways so every project suggested gets a small piece. However, you and some other members feel that this would not provide enough for any project to benefit. Someone else suggests not making a decision and putting all the money into an emergency account. You agree immediately. Others may push for using part of the money to accomplish something now. You can suggest that half goes into the emergency fund, and that the other half is used for a project. The group may agree and settle on a project quickly, recognizing that if they do not, nothing will get done.

Not reaching consensus may be a good time for a team-building exercise or to totally change the way things are done in the group, or you could simply ask members why they cannot find a point of consensus. Do any members have unspoken objectives or agendas that need to be aired? Again the most important idea here is to avoid allowing destructive confrontation. If this seems to happen, change the direction of discussion quickly. We stated before that groups should embrace differing ideas. Such disagreement enriches a group's process. But distinguish between useful confrontation and dysfunctional confrontation. Healthy disagreement is not the same as negative confrontation. Disagreement leads to airing diverse ideas. You want group members to express their viewpoints freely without negative consequences. But negative confrontation left unchecked leads to a lack of communication. The leader has to avoid this type of confrontation or stop it in its tracks, change direction, or air whatever frustrations group members are having and then move on. If negative confrontation is allowed to continue and fester, the group becomes dysfunctional, and healthy negotiations between members will not occur.

Appendix C

A PRIMER ON GIVING AND RECEIVING FEEDBACK

Giving Feedback

1. People generally do not react positively to feedback. They are naturally apprehensive about being evaluated. Also, they worry about how others will react to feedback.
2. People are lenient when it comes to evaluating themselves.
3. People are more likely to be open to positive feedback than to negative feedback because they naturally want to create and confirm a positive image of themselves. Conversely, they are likely to be threatened by, and likely to reject, negative feedback unless they believe they can benefit from it.
4. Feedback directs, motivates, and rewards behavior. It is the basis for development and career planning. Moreover, it contributes to building effective interpersonal relationships.
5. Effective feedback is clear, specific, frequent, immediate, and relevant to important job and learning behaviors (coaching).
6. Feedback is a dynamic process between source and recipient. It is a two-way interaction.
7. Constructive feedback:

   Doesn't blame people for negative outcomes.

   Doesn't compare people to others.

   Focuses on behaviors, not personal characteristics.

   Attributes good performance to internal causes, such as the subordinate's effort and ability.

Adapted from London (2002).

Recognizes when an individual should be praised for positive outcomes.

Concentrates on how the recipient and source can both win.

Increases the recipient's sense of independence and self-control.

Encourages and reinforces a can-do attitude.

Increases goal clarity.

Challenges the recipient to do better or overcome barriers on his or her own.

Allows a controlled expression of feelings.

Leads to increased mutual trust and confidence.

8. Destructive feedback can be destructive to individuals' careers and self-esteem.

9. Feedback givers should vary their approach depending on the likely reaction. For instance, they should know who is likely to be defensive and be prepared. They should be alert to the tendency many people have to rate themselves positively. Managers should deliver feedback that matches employees' readiness to change. This will reduce stress and reduce the time needed to bring about change.

10. The more that self-ratings agree with ratings from others, the more that individuals are likely to see the feedback as valid. Self-other agreement may be increased by providing feedback more frequently and basing feedback on objective, measurable criteria.

11. Information is likely to be perceived more accurately and be accepted when it:

Comes from a source the recipient views as knowledgeable and trustworthy.

Comes soon after the behavior.

Is positive, frequent, and specific.

12. People who are low in conscientiousness, emotional stability, openness to experience, agreeableness, or extroversion may

need more time and attention in helping them use feedback than people who are high in these personality variables. Those who are low in these characteristics are likely to be defensive.

13. Feedback is inextricably linked to goal setting, the means by which feedback motivates change. Ongoing feedback helps individuals calibrate their degree of goal accomplishment and the level of effort needed to reach the goal.

14. Individuals must participate in setting their own goals. Participation leads to commitment to the goals. Assigned goals do not work in every setting.

15. In conducting a formal performance review discussion:

> Focus on major responsibilities and performance standards.
>
> Identify causes for poor performance.
>
> Explain the purpose of the review meeting.
>
> Ask the recipient to summarize his or her accomplishments and developmental needs.
>
> Summarize accomplishments and developmental needs from your perspective.
>
> Reach agreement on what developmental steps should be taken.
>
> Initiate goal setting.

16. Principles for goal setting include encouraging employee participation and agreeing on specific goals. Employees do best when they perceive their goals as challenging, under their control, and achievable.

17. The appraisal and development cycle is a continuous process of improving employee performance that involves the subordinate. It rests on a foundation of clear communication, collaboration, goal setting, follow-up on goal accomplishment, and performance improvement. It involves (1) clarifying the employee's major responsibilities, (2) developing performance standards, (3) giving periodic performance feedback, (4) diagnosing performance problems and coaching in ways to improve, and (5) reviewing overall performance.

18. In-the-moment coaching can be a highly effective way to change behavior because it is immediate and closely tied to actual behaviors that can be discussed.

Receiving Feedback

1. We are more likely to change our behavior when we accept others' evaluations of weaknesses.

2. Our self-perceptions tend to agree substantially with the way we believe others see us. However, agreement between our self-perceptions and the way we are actually viewed by others is much lower. Nevertheless, self-perceptions can change with direct feedback.

3. Our personality affects how we react to feedback. People are more motivated to use feedback for development when they are conscientious, low in anxiety, and high in self-efficacy (the feeling of being able to make positive things happen).

4. Feedback seeking can be used to gather accurate information about oneself or as a technique to control what others think of you.

5. In receiving feedback, as at other times, people should be alert to their impression management behavior and the image they project. Impression management techniques include such assertive behaviors as ingratiation, intimidation, or self-promotion and defensive behaviors such as apologies, restitution, and disclaimers.

Group Feedback

Group feedback is valuable in informing group members about the performance of the group as a whole. This is appropriate when there is information about the group's performance and group members are interdependent. Group goals should be established during group discussion. With sufficient care, the group setting can be useful for giving feedback to individuals.

Group members may need help in accurately recognizing group accomplishments and failures. In particular, they tend to avoid blaming the group as a whole for a failure. They are more likely to identify individual members as the cause of group failure rather than hold the group collectively accountable. People who have more experience working with groups are more likely to hold the group as a whole accountable (Naquin & Tynan, 2003).

Team effectiveness depends on team members' developing shared mental models that facilitate coordination. Shared mental models include expectations about behaviors and skill levels, awareness of team members' knowledge and skills, and a shared understanding of the task and goals. Explicit communication about expectations and goals at the outset promotes the development of shared mental models. Feedback about behaviors and performance during the task enhances the development of these models and facilitates coordination and task accomplishment. Inaccurate expectations and feedback will thwart shared understanding and the ability of the group to coordinate their work.

In the future, we can expect abundant feedback from objective, technology-based sources of information. This poses the challenge of developing useful computer-based modes for involving people in self-management for continuous performance improvement. We will also find that people are increasingly responsible for assessment of their own skills, evaluation of opportunities and needs, and acquiring the skills and knowledge they require for continued success. Finally, we can expect a feedback-friendly or feedback-oriented culture in which group members are comfortable with giving and receiving feedback, and feedback is an integral part of the performance management process. A feedback-oriented culture can be developed by (1) enhancing the quality of feedback, (2) emphasizing the importance of feedback in the group, and (3) providing support for using feedback.

References

Absolute majority. (2006, June 29). In *Wikipedia, The Free Encyclopedia*. Retrieved July 25, 2006, from http://en.wikipedia.org/w/index.php?title=Absolute_majority&oldid=61256787.

Argote, L. (1999). *Organizational learning: Creating, retaining, and transferring knowledge*. Norwell, MA: Kluwer.

Arrow, H., McGrath, J. E., & Berdahl, J. L. (2000). *Small groups as complex systems: Formation, coordination, development, and adaptation*. Thousand Oaks, CA: Sage.

Aube, C., & Rousseau, V. (2005). Team goal commitment and team effectiveness: The role of task interdependence and supportive behaviors. *Group Dynamics: Theory, Research and Practice, 9*, 189–204.

Bales, R. F. (1950). *Interaction process analysis*. Reading, MA: Addison-Wesley.

Bass, B. M. (1998). *Transformational leadership: Industrial, military, and educational impact*. Mahwah, NJ: Erlbaum.

Bateman, T. S., & Crant, J. M. (2003). The proactive component of organizational behavior: A measure and correlates. *Journal of Organizational Behavior, 14*, 103–118.

Baumeister, R. F. (1982). A self-presentational view of social phenomena. *Psychological Bulletin, 91*, 3–26.

Bunderson, S., & Sutcliffe, K. (2003). Management team learning orientation and business unit performance. *Journal of Applied Psychology, 88*, 552–560.

Communication Styles. (1999). Eden Prairie, MN: Wilson Learning Corporation.

Cooke, N. J., Kiekel, P. A., Salas, E., Stout, R., Bowers, C., & Cannon-Bowers, J. (2003). Measuring team knowledge: A window to the cognitive underpinnings of team performance. *Group Dynamics: Theory, Research, and Practice, 7*, 179–199.

Dahlin, K.I.B., Weingart, L. R., & Hinds, P. J. (2006). Team diversity and information use. *Academy of Management Journal, 48*, 1107–1123.

DeShon, R. P., Kozlowski, S.W.J., Schmidt, A. M., Milner, K. R., & Wiechmann, D. (2004). A multiple-goal, multilevel model of feedback effects on the regulation of individual and team performance. *Journal of Applied Psychology, 89,* 1035–1056.

Drach-Zahavy, A., & Somech, A. (2001). Understanding team innovation: The role of team processes and structures. *Group Dynamics: Theory, Research, and Practice, 5,* 111–123.

Edmondson, A. (1999). Psychological safety and learning behavior in work teams. *Administrative Science Quarterly, 44,* 350–383.

Ericksen, J., & Dyer, L. (2004). Right from the start: Exploring the effects of early team events on subsequent project team development and performance. *Administrative Science Quarterly, 49,* 438–471.

Fisher, R., Ury, W., & Patton, B. (1991). *Getting to yes: Negotiating agreement without giving in.* New York: Penguin Books.

Fletcher, A. (2002). *FireStarter youth power curriculum: Guidebook.* Olympia, WA: Freechild Project.

Freedman, A. M. (2000). Multigroup representation: Representative teams and teams of representatives. *Consulting Psychology Journal: Practice and Research, 52,* 63–81.

Gersick, C. (1989). Marking time: Predictable transitions in task groups. *Academy of Management Journal, 32,* 274–309.

Hackman, J. R. (2002). *Leading teams: Setting the stage for great performance.* Boston: Harvard Business School Press.

Hackman, J. R. (2003). Learning more by crossing levels: Evidence from airplanes, hospitals, and orchestras. *Journal of Organizational Behavior, 24,* 905–922.

Hackman, J. R., & Wageman, R. (2005). A theory of team coaching. *Academy of Management Review, 30,* 269–287.

Henningsen, D. D., Henningsen, M.L.M., Eden, J., & Cruz, M. G. (2006). Examining the symptoms of groupthink and retrospective sensemaking. *Small Group Research, 37,* 36–64.

Hirschfeld, R. R., Jordan, M. H., Field, H. S., & Armenakis, A. A. (2005). Teams' female representation and perceived potency as inputs to team outcomes in a predominantly male field setting. *Personnel Psychology, 58,* 893–824.

Hogan, R., & Kaiser, R. B. (2005). What we know about leadership. *Review of General Psychology, 9,* 169–180.

Janis, I. L. (1972). *Victims of groupthink.* Boston: Houghton Mifflin.

Jermier, J. M., & Kerr, S. (1997). Substitutes for leadership: Their meaning and measurement. *Leadership Quarterly, 8,* 95–101.

Johnson, L. K. (2005, September). Give them a challenge they can't resist. *Harvard Management Update.* Retrieved Oct. 5, 2005, from http://harvardbusinessonlinehbsp.harvard.edu.

Katz-Navon, T. Y., & Erez, M. (2005). When collective- and self-efficacy affect team performance: The role of task interdependence. *Small Group Research, 36,* 437–465.

Keller, R. (2006). Transformational leadership, initiative structure, and substitutes for leadership: A longitudinal study of research and development project team performance. *Journal of Applied Psychology, 91*, 202–210.

Kilman, R., & Thomas, K. (1975). Interpersonal conflict handling behavior as reflections of Jungian personality dimensions. *Psychological Reports, 37*, 971–980.

Kozlowski, S.W.J., & Ilgen, D. R. (in press). Enhancing the effectiveness of work groups and teams. *Psychological Science in the Public Interest.*

Lencioni, P. (2002). *The five dysfunctions of a team.* San Francisco: Jossey-Bass.

LePine, J. (2005). Adaptation of teams in response to unforeseen change: Effects of goal difficulty and team composition in terms of cognitive ability and goal orientation. *Journal of Applied Psychology, 90*, 1153–1167.

Lewis, K. (2003). Measuring transactive memory systems in the field: Scale development and validation. *Journal of Applied Psychology, 88*(4), 587–604.

Lewis, K. (2004). Knowledge and performance in knowledge-worker teams: A longitudinal study of transactive memory systems. *Management Science, 50*, 1519–1533.

Lewis, K., Lange, D., & Gillis, L. (2005). Transactive memory systems, learning, and learning transfer. *Organization Science, 16*, 581–598.

London, M. (2002). *Job feedback* (2nd ed). Mahwah, NJ: Erlbaum.

London, M. M. (1982). *Music and language: An ethnographic study of music and learning and interpreting situations.* Unpublished doctoral dissertation, Rutgers University.

Mannix, E., & Neale, M. A. (2005). What differences make a difference? The promise and reality of diverse teams in organizations. *Psychological Science in the Public Interest, 6*, 31–55.

Marks, M. A., Mathieu, J. E., DeChurch, L. A., Panzer, F. J., & Alonso, A. (2005). Teamwork in multiteam systems. *Journal of Applied Psychology, 90*(5), 964–971.

Marks, M. A., Mathieu, J. E., & Zaccaro, S. J. (2001). A temporarily based framework and taxonomy of team processes. *Academy of Management Review, 26*, 356–376.

Marks, M. A., Sabella, M. J., Burke, C. S., & Zaccaro, S. J. (2002). The impact of cross-training on team effectiveness. *Journal of Applied Psychology, 87*, 3–13.

Martin, A. (2006, January). Complex challenges and the new leadership. *Leading effectively.* Retrieved Feb. 2, 2006, from http://www.ccl.org.

Mathieu, J. E., Gilson, L. L., & Ruddy, T. M. (2006). Empowerment and team effectiveness: An empirical test of an integrated model. *Journal of Applied Psychology, 91*, 97–108.

Mayer, J. D., & Salovey, P. (1997). What is emotional intelligence? In P. Salovey & D. Sluyter (Eds.), *Emotional development and emotional intelligence: Implications for educators* (pp. 3–31). New York: Basic Books.

McKenna, P., & Maister, D. (2002). *First among equals: How to manage a group of professionals*. New York: Free Press.

Messina, J. J., & Messina, C. M. (2006). *Tools for personal growth: Building trust*. Retrieved July 26, 2006, from http://www.coping.org/growth/trust.htm.

Myers, N. D., Feltz, D. L., & Short, S. E. (2004). Collective efficacy and team performance: A longitudinal study of collegiate football teams. *Group Dynamics: Theory, Research, and Practice, 8*, 126–138.

Naquin, C. E., & Tynan, R. O. (2003). The team halo effect: Why teams are not blamed for their failures. *Journal of Applied Psychology, 88*, 332–340.

Niziol, F., & Free, K. (2005). The team start-up: A scripted approach to facilitating the start of an effective work team. In S. Schuman (Ed.), *IAF handbook of group facilitation* (pp. 315–334). San Francisco: Jossey-Bass.

Pearsall, M. J., & Ellis, A.P.J. (2006). The effects of critical team member assertiveness on team performance and satisfaction. *Journal of Management, 32*, 575–594.

Platts, D. E. (2003). *The Findhorn book of building trust in groups*. Forres, Scotland: Findhorn Press.

Polzer, J., Swann, W., & Milton, L. (2002). Capitalizing on diversity: Interpersonal congruence in small work groups. *Administrative Science Quarterly, 47*, 296–324.

Quinn, R. E. (1988). *Beyond rational management: Mastering the paradoxes and competing demands of high performance*. San Francisco: Jossey-Bass.

Raelin, J. (2006). Does action learning promote collaborative leadership? *Academy of Management Learning and Education, 5*, 152–168.

Riggio, R. E., Riggio, H. R., Salinas, C., & Cole, E. J. (2003). The role of social and emotional communication skills in leader emergence and effectiveness. *Group Dynamics: Theory, Research, and Practice, 7*, 83–103.

Robin, A., & Foster, S. (2003). *Negotiating parent-adolescent conflict: A behavioral-family systems approach*. New York: Guilford Press.

Rogelberg, S. G., Leach, D. J., Warr, P. B., & Burnfield, J. L. (2006). "Not another meeting!" Are meeting time demands related to employee well-being? *Journal of Applied Psychology, 91*, 86–96.

Schwarz, R. (2002). *The skilled facilitator: A comprehensive resource for consultants, facilitators, managers, trainers, and coaches*. San Francisco: Jossey-Bass.

Schwarz, R. (2005a). The skilled facilitator approach. In S. Schuman (Ed.), *IAF handbook of group facilitation* (pp. 21–34). San Francisco: Jossey-Bass.

Schwarz, R. (2005b). Using facilitative skills in different roles. In R. Schwarz, A. Davidson, P. Carlson, & S. McKinney (Eds.), *The skilled facilitator fieldbook: Tips, tools, and tested methods for consultants, facilitators, managers, trainers, and coaches* (pp. 27–32). San Francisco: Jossey-Bass.

Sessa, V. I., & London, M. (2006). *Continuous learning*. Mahwah, NJ: Erlbaum.

Sevier, R. (2005). Anatomy of a successful team. *University Business, 9*, 23–24.

Simsek, Z., Veiga, J. F., Lubatkin, M. H., & Dino, R. N. (2005). Modeling the multilevel determinants of top management team behavioral integration. *Academy of Management Journal, 48*, 69–84.

Smith, G. (2001). Group development: A review of the literature and a commentary on future research directions. *Group Facilitation: A Research and Applications Journal, 3*. Retrieved July 27, 2006, from http://www.findarticles.com/p/articles/mi_qa3954/is_200104/ai_n8943660.

Stockton, R., Morran, K., & Berardi, M. (2004). An investigation of group leaders' intentions. *Group Dynamics: Theory, Research, and Practice, 8*, 196–206.

Supermajority. (2006, May 8). In *Wikipedia, The Free Encyclopedia*. Retrieved July 26, 2006, from http://en.wikipedia.org/w/index.php?title=Supermajority&oldid=52219035.

Tuckman, B. W. (1965). Developmental sequence in small groups. *Psychological Bulletin, 63*, 384–399.

Tuckman, B. W., & Jensen, M.A.C. (1977). Stages of small group development revisited. *Group and Organizational Studies, 2*, 419–427.

Wegner, D. M. (1987). Transactive memory: A contemporary analysis of the group mind. In B. Mullen & G. R. Goethals (Eds.), *Theories of group behavior* (pp. 185–208). New York: Springer-Verlag.

West, E. (1999). *The big book of icebreakers: Quick, fun activities for energizing meetings and workshops*. New York: McGraw-Hill.

West, M. (1996). Innovation in top management teams. *Journal of Applied Psychology, 81*, 678–693.

West, M. A. (2002). Sparkling fountains or stagnant ponds: An integrative model of creativity and innovation implementation in work groups. *Applied Psychology: An International Review, 51*, 355–424.

Wong, S. S. (2004). Distal and local group learning: Performance trade-offs and tensions. *Organizational Science, 15*, 645–656.

Zaccaro, S. J., Hildebrand, H., & Shuffler, M. (in press). The leader's role in group learning. In V. I. Sessa & M. London (Eds.), *Group learning*. Mahwah, NJ: Erlbaum.

Index